An Ethical Compass

Connecting the Inner and Outer Worlds

RP Sidgen

SIDGEN BOOKS
INDIA

An Ethical Compass
Connecting the Inner and Outer Worlds
by R.P. Sidgen

This is a work of original poetry and philosophy connecting to the historical evidence to prove what is said in the poetry is true and universal. Any resemblance to actual events, places, or persons, living or dead, is purely coincidental.

First Edition: 2025

Published by Sidgen Books

ISBN: 978-93-342-7951-1

This is a work of non-fiction. The views and interpretations expressed within are those of the author. While every effort has been made to ensure accuracy, the author and publisher assume no responsibility for errors or omissions.

For permissions, inquiries, or more information, contact:

admin@sidgenbooks.com

Printed in India

www.sidgenbooks.com

Contents

Preface

Life is an ever-unfolding journey, shaped by the interplay of thought, experience, and inner reflection. Across time, humanity has sought answers to the deeper questions of existence—what it means to live ethically, to think clearly, and to act with purpose. An Ethical Compass is a humble attempt to explore those timeless truths through poetic reflections that bridge the wisdom of the past with the introspection of the present.

A significant inspiration for this work is the celebrated Telugu poet and philosopher Sri Yogi Vemana, whose verses—simple in form yet profound in meaning—have enlightened generations. Several poems in this collection are free English translations, interpretations, or creative adaptations of Vemana's original insights. While not exact replicas, they carry forward his essence—his fearless questioning of social norms, his reverence for virtue, and his unwavering commitment to truth.

This book is not intended as a scholarly translation but as a tribute to his ethical vision. Through these pages, I have sought to breathe new life into age-old values, preserving their spirit while giving them a contemporary voice.

Each chapter invites reflection on the universal themes of human life—virtue, impermanence, compassion, self-awareness, and the search for meaning. These thoughts are not bound by time or culture; they are seeds of wisdom meant to be planted in the hearts of those who seek clarity in a chaotic world.

This is not a book to rush through. It is a quiet companion for your reflective moments, a mirror that may at times challenge, at times console, and often awaken the deeper voice within. May it guide you, gently and earnestly, as you trace your own path—anchored by an ethical compass.

— R.P. Sidgen

Acknowledgments

Writing this book has been a journey of exploration, reflection, and growth—one that would not have been possible without the support, encouragement, and wisdom of many.

First and foremost, I express my deepest gratitude to those who have inspired me to think deeply and question fearlessly. Every conversation, every challenge, and every lesson has shaped the ideas within these pages.

To my teachers, mentors, and guides—thank you for instilling in me a love for wisdom and the courage to seek it. Your influence extends far beyond words.

To my family and friends—your unwavering support and belief in me have been a source of strength. Your encouragement, patience, and understanding have helped bring this book to life.

To my readers—this book is for you. Whether you seek answers or simply wish to reflect on life's mysteries, I hope these pages offer you something meaningful. Thank you for embarking on this journey with me.

And finally, to the unseen forces of life—the moments of clarity, the struggles that teach, and the whispers of wisdom that guide us all. Without them, this book would not exist.

With gratitude,

— R.P. Sidgen

Chapter 1

Virtue and Character

Virtue shapes the foundation of a strong character. It is not defined by external recognition but by inner integrity. A person's true nature is revealed in moments of challenge, where honesty, kindness, and resilience stand as tests of character. Those who uphold virtue remain unshaken by circumstances, while those who compromise it eventually face consequences. Character is built through consistent actions, not occasional gestures. It is the essence that defines trust, respect, and honor in society, proving that true strength lies not in power or wealth, but in the unwavering commitment to ethical values. Through historical figures like Socrates and Confucius, we learn that integrity and moral courage define a person more than status or wealth. True character is tested in times of adversity, where virtue stands resilient against corruption.

Silver and tin appear alike in a fleeting view,
Yet their worth reveals the difference, sharp and true.
As virtue stands apart from the false hue,
Truth shines through the veil, eternal and new.

Truth vs. Illusion

Things are not always as they seem. Silver and tin appear alike, but their value differs significantly. Similarly, people or situations may project deceptive appearances, but their true nature eventually emerges. Virtue, like Silver's divine quality and value, stands apart from falsehood. Truth is timeless, shining through even when masked by illusions. The poem encourages discernment, urging us to look beyond the surface. A virtuous life, anchored in truth, withstands the trials of deception, while the false eventually crumbles when exposed.

A young prince was captivated by a gleaming gem sold by a merchant. His advisor tested it against sunlight, revealing it as a worthless crystal. Later, the prince found a dull-looking stone that sparkled brilliantly under light—a true diamond. The advisor taught, "Like tin and Silver, truth is revealed through tests, not appearances." The prince learned to value discernment over assumptions.

On a December day in 1955, Rosa Parks boarded a bus in Montgomery, Alabama. She was an ordinary woman—a seamstress—sitting quietly on her way home. But when asked to give up her seat for a white passenger, she said one word: "No." That simple act of defiance was the spark that ignited the Civil Rights Movement.

Rosa Parks didn't shout or stage a dramatic protest. Her quiet courage proved that you don't need to look strong to be strong. Her virtue lay in her resolve, her unwavering belief in equality, and her willingness to stand up—literally—for what was right. Her story reminds us that true strength isn't always loud or visible. It's in the quiet decisions, the moments when we choose principle over convenience, and the times we stand firm even when the world tells us to sit down. Rosa Parks proved that virtue, not appearance, changes the world.

"Appearances are deceptive; the truth is constant."

A noble soul in a family tree,
Like incense, spreads fragrance free.
Uplifts the lineage with dignity,
An emblem of virtue, for all to see.

Noble Influence

A virtuous person is like incense, whose fragrance uplifts everyone around. Their presence enhances the dignity of their family and society. A single noble soul can transform an entire lineage, bringing honor and respect. This poem reminds us of the power of virtue to leave a lasting legacy. Just as incense's aroma spreads far and wide, a person's goodness impacts lives beyond their immediate circle. Being a beacon of integrity enriches not just oneself but also inspires others, setting an example for generations to emulate.

A humble teacher in a small village taught children without expecting rewards. Years later, his students became successful and returned to honor him. The teacher's virtues spread through his students, uplifting families and the community. Like sandalwood, his influence left a lasting legacy.

During the Crimean War, Florence Nightingale transformed the grim battlefield hospitals into places of hope and healing. Known as the "Lady with the Lamp," she walked through the wards at night, her presence a beacon of comfort to wounded soldiers. But Nightingale's influence went far beyond her bedside. She introduced hygiene practices that drastically reduced mortality rates and laid the foundation for modern nursing.

Nightingale's story is a testament to the power of noble influence. Her quiet dedication not only saved lives but also inspired generations to pursue compassionate service. She showed that one person's commitment to a noble cause can ripple across the world. Her legacy teaches us that true power doesn't lie in titles or wealth but in the ability to uplift others and transform lives.

"A good tree bears good fruit."

A virtue born of a pure, selfless mind,
Even in small deeds, grows divine.
A mighty banyan springs from a seed confined,
Its roots entwined with life's design.

The Power of Virtue

Virtue, born from a selfless mind, holds immense potential, no matter how small the act. Just as a mighty banyan tree springs from a tiny seed, good deeds, though seemingly insignificant, grow into something profound and enduring. Virtue connects lives, fosters growth, and becomes an integral part of existence. The poem reminds us to nurture kindness and compassion, understanding that even the smallest gestures of selflessness can have a transformative and far-reaching impact, intertwining with the fabric of life like the roots of a banyan tree.

A farmer planted a single banyan seed near his barren land. Over decades, the tree grew massive, offering shade and shelter to villagers, animals, and travelers. When asked why he planted it, the farmer replied, "A small act of care can grow into a blessing for many." Inspired, the villagers began planting trees, transforming their land into a green haven. Like the banyan, selfless actions can flourish, enriching lives for generations.

In Nazi-occupied Poland, a woman named Irena Sendler quietly walked the streets of Warsaw, carrying nothing but a nurse's bag and a heart full of resolve. While the world outside the Jewish Ghetto turned a blind eye, she saw suffering—children starving, families torn apart, and hope withering like a plant in a drought.

Irena, working for the Social Welfare Department, had access to the ghetto. She smuggled in food and medicine, but soon, she realized that saving lives meant something greater. One by one, she began rescuing Jewish children, carrying them out hidden in baskets, toolboxes, or even beneath stretchers. Some she led through secret underground tunnels, while others she disguised as Christian orphans.

Every life she saved was a seed of virtue. She wrote down each child's real name and new identity on thin strips of paper and buried them in glass jars under an apple tree—hoping that one day, these children could reunite with their families.

She saved 2,500 children—a number that seemed small against the vastness of war, but like a tiny seed, her virtue grew beyond measure. Arrested by the Nazis, she was tortured and sentenced to death, but even broken bones couldn't break her spirit. She escaped and continued her mission, never seeking recognition.

Years later, when her story resurfaced, she simply said, "I could have done more." But history knew better. Her selflessness, like the roots of a banyan tree, intertwined with the lives she saved, spreading kindness across generations.

Irena's story reminds us that virtue, no matter how small, has the power to transform the world. Like a single banyan seed growing into an eternal tree, every act of kindness we plant today will take root in the hearts of tomorrow.

"From small beginnings come great things."

A small favor to virtue seems immense,
While the wicked repay good with offense.
Gratitude depends on moral sense,
For the heart's value reflects its conscience.

The Value of Gratitude and Virtue

This poem compares how acts of kindness are perceived by different individuals, suggesting that a small favor is immense to a virtuous person but insignificant to the wicked, who may even repay good with offense. Gratitude is not a universal reaction; it depends on the moral character of the individual. The poem underscores that one's ability to recognize kindness and respond with appreciation is a reflection of their inner goodness, and those with a noble heart will always value good deeds, regardless of their size.

A kind woman helped a poor beggar by offering him food and shelter for a night. He, deeply grateful, thanked her profusely and promised to repay her kindness one day. However, when a wealthy man offered her a much larger sum for the same favor, she accepted it without hesitation. The beggar, witnessing this, felt betrayed and furious. The woman explained, "Gratitude is not measured by what is given, but by the heart that receives it." The beggar understood that the woman's true virtue was in her kindness, not in the value of what was offered. He vowed to repay her kindness by spreading generosity to others.

During the Nazi occupation of the Netherlands, Anne Frank's family went into hiding to avoid arrest. The Frank family was helped by a group of brave individuals who risked their lives to provide shelter and support. Anne's father, Otto Frank, after the war, publicly expressed his immense gratitude to these helpers for their selfless courage, despite the constant danger they faced.

This story of gratitude in the face of such peril highlights the importance of acknowledging those who help us, especially in times of crisis. Otto Frank's recognition of their bravery serves as a reminder that gratitude can offer healing and recognition in a world often marked by ingratitude. It contrasts the selfishness of those who might ignore or dismiss acts of kindness with the humility and strength of those who openly express thanks. Gratitude, in its purest form, is both a powerful tribute to others and a reflection of our own values.

Read the following stories and find the contrast in the characters.

A Heart That Saw Immense Value in Small Acts

Abdul Sattar Edhi, a humble man from Pakistan, dedicated his life to serving the poor. He started with nothing—just a small table on a Karachi street, where he sat, collecting donations for the needy.

One day, a child approached him with a single rupee, a trivial amount to many. But Edhi's eyes lit up as if he had received a fortune. He thanked the boy wholeheartedly and placed the coin in his charity box, saying, "This is wealth greater than any gold, for it comes from a pure heart."

Over time, Edhi built Pakistan's largest humanitarian foundation, caring for orphans, abandoned infants, and the destitute. To him, no act of kindness was too small—it was all precious and meaningful.

A Favor That Ended in Betrayal

Julius Caesar, the ruler of Rome, was known for his generosity, even toward those who had once opposed him. Among his closest friends was Brutus, a man whom he had forgiven and favored despite past conflicts.

When political conspirators plotted against Caesar, Brutus joined them. Though Caesar had given him power and trusted him like a son, Brutus repaid this kindness with a dagger to the heart. "Et tu, Brute?"—Caesar's last words—were not just of betrayal but of disbelief that even generosity could be answered with cruelty.

"Gratitude is the sign of noble souls."

The mean stay mean, though they read and hear,
Coal stays black, untouched by milk's veneer.
Deep-rooted nature defies all reform,
Habits ingrained resist every norm.

They may learn much, yet remain the same,
For nature outlives knowledge or name.
A donkey with scents is a donkey still,
Essence is fate, not sharpened by will.

The Immutability of Nature

It is very difficult to change ingrained habits and characteristics. Just as coal remains black no matter how much it is handled, and no amount of milk can make it white, people with deep-rooted vices or negative qualities cannot be easily transformed. The poem suggests that nature, whether it's an object or a person's personality, is often resistant to change, and while external factors can influence behavior, a person's essence or ingrained habits are difficult to alter unless they choose to change from within.

A rich merchant invited a famous philosopher to his home, hoping to change his wife's greedy nature. The philosopher suggested that she focus on charity and kindness, but the merchant's wife, stubborn and materialistic, refused. The merchant was frustrated, but the philosopher told him, "Coal can be polished, but it will still remain black unless it chooses to burn clean." The merchant learned that true change requires internal willingness. He realized that no matter how much he tried, his wife's nature would not shift unless she herself decided to change. He understood that change must come from within.

Incurable Vices

Al Capone, the notorious gangster, amassed wealth, power, and influence during the Prohibition era, but he never shed his deeply ingrained criminal tendencies. Even after his rise to fame and fortune, he continued his criminal activities, leading to his eventual downfall. Despite external changes in his circumstances, his inner vices—greed, violence, and dishonesty—remained unshakable, much like coal that remains black no matter how it is handled.

Capone's life is a stark reminder of the difficulty in breaking free from ingrained behaviors. Wealth and status might alter outward appearances, but they cannot cure the inner flaws that drive destructive choices. His story teaches us that true transformation comes from within, and no amount of external success can change a person who has not made the conscious decision to reform their character.

"A leopard cannot change its spots."

The Unchangeable Nature of Nero

In ancient Rome, a young boy named Nero was born into a privileged yet chaotic world. His mother, Agrippina, schemed and manipulated to place him on the throne, believing she could mold him into a wise and just emperor. She surrounded him with great philosophers, including the revered Seneca, who tirelessly taught him about virtue, restraint, and leadership.

At first, there was hope. Nero listened, pretended to be just, and showed flashes of promise. But beneath the surface, his true nature remained untouched—self-indulgent, cruel, and power-hungry. As he gained more control, his tutors' wisdom became mere background noise to his darker impulses.

Power only magnified his worst traits. He orchestrated the murder of his mother, exiled and forced Seneca to take his own life, and infamously watched Rome burn while playing his lyre, caring little for the people suffering around him. No amount of guidance, philosophy, or counsel could turn him into the noble emperor his advisors had hoped for.

Eventually, his tyranny led to his downfall. As enemies closed in, he was abandoned, left to take his own life—his last words being, "What an artist dies in me!" Even in death, he saw himself as a performer, not as the cruel ruler he had been.

A person's true nature, once formed, is difficult to change. Just as a donkey carrying fragrant scents remains the same, individuals with negative tendencies struggle to alter their inherent traits. Essence is shaped early and remains deeply rooted, resisting transformation despite external influences. This highlights the challenge of changing ingrained behaviors and the importance of early character development.

Unchanged Nature

King Richard III, despite his education and opportunity, could not escape his inherent ruthlessness. Known for his violent and manipulative nature, Richard's tyranny led to his eventual downfall at the Battle of Bosworth in 1485. Despite his rise to power, his nature remained unchanged, and it was his cruelty and ambition that ultimately led to his demise.

Richard III's story illustrates that some traits are deeply ingrained, and no amount of external circumstance can alter them. Even with the best opportunities for redemption, if a person's core nature is rooted in vice, they will often be led by those impulses to destruction. His life is a reminder that our nature—our tendencies, whether good or bad—shapes our destiny, regardless of external factors. The Battle of Bosworth served as the final reckoning for Richard III, proving that even kings **cannot outrun the consequences of their inherent nature.**

"You can't teach an old dog new tricks."

If your brother gives charity's reward,
You should not expect a share or regard.
Does his leg ache when yours is scarred?
True generosity asks not for a sword.

The True Weight of Generosity

True generosity is a deeply personal virtue that cannot be transferred, borrowed, or shared simply because of proximity to a charitable person. Many people fall into the misconception that they deserve recognition or rewards for good deeds performed by someone close to them. However, just as physical pain is unique to the person experiencing it, so too is the merit of kindness and charity. No one can feel another's pain entirely, nor can they claim a share in another's virtue without personal effort. True kindness is not about receiving validation or social approval; it is about giving selflessly, without expecting anything in return. A genuinely generous person does not give with the hope of being acknowledged or praised but rather because they believe in the act of giving itself.

In a small town, two childhood friends, Arjun and Rohan, grew up together. Arjun was always kind-hearted and often helped those in need. He donated food to the hungry, taught underprivileged children for free, and never hesitated to offer a helping hand.

Rohan, on the other hand, was not as charitable. However, he believed that being close to Arjun automatically made him virtuous as well. When people praised Arjun for his generosity, Rohan would proudly say, "We have done so much for this town."

One day, a poor old man came to Rohan, asking for help. Rohan, expecting that Arjun would handle it, replied, "Go to my friend Arjun; he always helps."

Hearing this, Arjun smiled and said, "Rohan, if you get injured, should I take the medicine for you? Will that heal your wound?"

Rohan was taken aback. "No, of course not," he said.

Arjun continued, "Then why do you believe that my kindness can replace yours? Just as pain is personal, so is generosity. If you wish to be seen as kind, you must act with kindness yourself."

Rohan realized his mistake. From that day, he stopped taking credit for Arjun's actions and started helping others in his own way.

The Illusion of Barrowed Virtue

During the Maurya Empire, Emperor Ashoka, after witnessing the horrors of war, transformed into a ruler who valued peace and compassion. He dedicated his life to spreading Buddhism, constructing hospitals, and ensuring the welfare of his people. His generosity and kindness became legendary.

One of his ministers, Subandhu, often claimed, "I am close to Emperor Ashoka. His virtue is mine as well." Though he himself had never performed any acts of kindness, he believed he was deserving of praise simply because he was part of the emperor's court.

One day, Ashoka overheard him. The emperor called for a large stone to be placed in the middle of the court and asked Subandhu to move it. The minister struggled but failed.

Ashoka then addressed him, "If you cannot carry this stone, why do you believe you can carry my virtue? Just as strength must be one's own, so must kindness."

Subandhu realized his folly and changed his ways, understanding that righteousness and generosity could not be borrowed—they had to be earned through action.

True generosity is a personal virtue, not something that can be shared or inherited. Just as one person's pain does not physically transfer to another, neither does the merit of good deeds. If we wish to be recognized for kindness, we must practice it ourselves rather than expecting a share of another's goodwill. True virtue is silent, selfless, and sincere.

"A Virtue Owned, Not Borrowed"

Tall stature, long beard, and handsome guise,
Without charity, greatness lies in disguise.
A buffalo's size won't make it wise,
For virtue lies not in form's rise.

True Greatness Lies in Virtue, Not in Appearance

True greatness is not about outward appearances, such as tall stature or a handsome guise. These are superficial attributes that do not define a person's true worth. The comparison of a buffalo's size to wisdom illustrates that physical form has no bearing on intellectual or moral strength. True virtue lies within, not in the external traits. The poem emphasizes that greatness is found in one's actions and character, not in the superficial qualities that may attract attention.

Once, there was a blacksmith named, who admired himself for his broad shoulders and strong arms. He often boasted, "My strength makes me the greatest in this village!" He would lift heavy objects effortlessly and expected people to respect him for his physical power.

One day, a frail old potter challenged him, "Strength alone does not make a man great. Let's see who can make something truly valuable." The blacksmith laughed at the challenge but agreed. He forged a massive iron statue, while the old potter carefully shaped a delicate clay pot.

When the village gathered to judge, a wise elder said, "The statue is impressive, but it serves no purpose. Though fragile, the pot carries water for the people. True worth lies in service, not just strength."

The blacksmith felt humbled and understood that greatness isn't in muscle but in meaningful actions. From that day, he used his strength to help others, earning true respect.

True Generosity

Andrew Carnegie's rise from poverty to becoming one of the wealthiest men in history is a testament to the American dream. However, it wasn't his fortune that defined his legacy, but rather how he chose to use it. After amassing wealth through his steel empire, Carnegie became one of the most famous philanthropists of his time. He believed that the rich had a moral obligation to redistribute their wealth for the benefit of society. Carnegie funded the creation of over 2,500 public libraries, making knowledge accessible to people from all walks of life. He also donated vast sums to the development of educational institutions and scientific research, establishing foundations that continue to impact the world today. However, his philanthropy wasn't without criticism. Many believed his generosity was a way to secure his legacy and divert attention from the harsh working conditions in his factories.

Yet, Carnegie's story is still one of true generosity—he gave back to society in ways that continue to benefit countless individuals. His wealth, once amassed through industry and hard work, was transformed into something that elevated communities, proving that true generosity goes beyond amassing riches—it is about how those riches are used to bring lasting positive change.

"Don't judge a book by its cover."

Long service to an unworthy master,
Is chasing shadows, courting disaster.
Like milking a barren cow, hopes shatter,
For empty pursuits lead to nothing thereafter.

The Futility of Serving an Unworthy Master

This poem speaks about the futility of serving an unworthy or ungrateful master. It uses the metaphor of milking a barren cow, suggesting that no matter how much effort is put into an unworthy cause, it will lead to nothing. The poem emphasizes the idea that empty pursuits, especially those driven by vanity or selfishness, are ultimately fruitless. It calls for mindfulness in choosing where to invest time and energy, as serving a cause or person that offers no real value will only lead to disappointment.

A young servant worked tirelessly for his master, believing that his efforts would one day be rewarded. However, his master was cruel and ungrateful, taking advantage of the servant's loyalty. One day, the servant approached an elder, asking why his hard work brought no reward. The elder replied, "Milking a barren cow is a wasted effort. You cannot get milk from what is empty." The servant realized he had been chasing after something that would never bear fruit. He left his master and sought work with a kind and just man, finding fulfillment in service that was valued. He learned that serving a worthy cause brings true reward.

The Betrayal of General Yue Fei
– A Loyal Servant to an Unworthy Emperor

During the 12th century, China was under attack from the Jurchen invaders, and the Song Dynasty was struggling to defend its lands. One of the greatest generals of the time, Yue Fei, was fiercely loyal to Emperor Gaozong. He led his troops with unwavering dedication, winning battle after battle, and was on the verge of reclaiming lost territories. His motto was "Serve the country with utmost loyalty."

However, back in the imperial court, corrupt officials, led by Chancellor Qin Hui, saw Yue Fei's growing influence as a threat. They manipulated Emperor Gaozong, convincing him that the general was becoming too powerful and might overthrow him. Despite Yue Fei's loyalty, he was recalled from the battlefield, imprisoned on false charges, and later executed.

Years later, the emperor realized his grave mistake, but by then, the kingdom had lost its greatest warrior. Today, Yue Fei is remembered as a symbol of loyalty and patriotism, while Qin Hui is despised as a traitor.

Serving an unworthy master, no matter how loyal and hardworking you are, can lead to ruin. True service should be given to those who appreciate and value it.

Sometimes, even the kings fall victim to the deeds done by the foolish caretakers.

Tsar Nicholas II's reliance on Rasputin is one of the most infamous examples of misplaced trust in history. Rasputin, a mystic and self-proclaimed holy man, gained significant influence over the Russian royal family in the early 20th century. He was especially close to Tsarina Alexandra, who believed Rasputin had healing powers that could cure her son, Tsarevich Alexei, who suffered from hemophilia. Despite Rasputin's dubious background and controversial actions, Nicholas II trusted him and allowed him to wield significant influence over the Russian court. Rasputin's involvement in the royal family's affairs, including appointments to government positions, undermined the credibility of the monarchy and led to widespread disillusionment among the Russian people. Many believed that Rasputin's influence was one of the factors that led to the fall of the Romanov dynasty and the Russian Revolution. Nicholas II's unwavering loyalty to Rasputin, despite mounting evidence of his lack of merit, ultimately damaged his reign. Rasputin's role in the Russian court is a powerful reminder of the dangers of relying on unqualified individuals for important decisions, and how misplaced trust can erode the credibility of even the most powerful leaders.

"A fool's errand brings no gain."

The man who admits he knows not is wise,
He who boasts of knowledge earns despise.
Silence reveals wisdom in disguise,
For humility speaks truth, no lies.

Humility Over Boasting

The wisdom found in humility and the foolishness of boasting. A person who admits their ignorance is considered wise, while those who boast about their knowledge earn the disdain of others. Silence, humility, and a willingness to learn are the true signs of wisdom, as they reveal the ability to acknowledge one's limitations and seek truth without pride or pretense.

A young scholar boasted of his knowledge, always claiming that he knew everything. One day, he met an old sage who had lived a life of wisdom and experience. The sage remained silent during their conversation, not boasting or speaking of his knowledge. The young scholar grew impatient and said, "Why don't you share your wisdom?" The sage replied, "True wisdom is not about speaking of what you know, but in knowing when to listen and learn." The young scholar realized that his constant boasting had closed the doors to true learning. He learned that silence and humility open the path to true wisdom.

Wisdom in Silence

The Dalai Lama, a spiritual leader renowned for his kindness and wisdom, has often spoken about the importance of silence and reflection in cultivating wisdom.

Throughout his life, he has emphasized that true understanding comes not from the rush of words or external achievements, but from quiet contemplation and the ability to listen deeply to both others and oneself. The Dalai Lama's approach to wisdom is rooted in the belief that silence fosters clarity, enabling individuals to connect with their inner selves and with the world around them in a meaningful way. In a world often filled with noise and distractions, the Dalai Lama's teachings urge us to embrace stillness, allowing us to process our thoughts and emotions before acting or speaking. Wisdom, he believes, grows not from boasting or the loudness of one's voice, but from the humility of silence. His teachings challenge the modern notion that speaking loudly or constantly is a sign of strength or wisdom. Rather, true strength lies in the ability to remain silent, reflect, and approach life with calmness and understanding. The Dalai Lama's example serves as a powerful reminder that sometimes the most profound insights come not from speaking, but from listening and reflecting in silence.

"He who knows does not speak. He who speaks does not know."

A pig births many; the elephant, just one.
Isn't one noble soul's work well done?
Greatness shines brighter than the sun,
For quality far exceeds quantity's run.

The Power of One Over Many

True greatness is not measured by the quantity of one's achievements or offspring, but by their quality. A pig may give birth to many, but an elephant produces just one, and that one is far more valuable due to its significance. In life, one noble, wise, or virtuous act or person is worth more than countless lesser ones. Greatness shines not through numbers, but through the impact and value of what is created or achieved.

A poor farmer worked tirelessly to raise a flock of sheep, each one valuable in its own way. However, his neighbor, a wise man, raised just one horse. Over time, the horse proved far more valuable than the entire flock of sheep, helping the farmer plow his fields, transport goods, and even defend his farm from thieves. The farmer learned that it is not the quantity of things that matter, but the quality and the impact of one's choices. The wise neighbor had focused on the one thing that could change his life, and that one horse made all the difference.

Quality Over Quantity

Albert Einstein's theory of relativity revolutionized the way we understand the universe, proving that quality far outweighs quantity in the realm of intellectual achievement. Einstein spent years contemplating and developing his groundbreaking theories, which fundamentally changed physics, yet he produced fewer theories than many of his contemporaries.

His singular achievement, however, left an indelible mark on science, proving that one profound idea can have a more significant impact than countless minor contributions. The theory of relativity, with its complex equations and the insight it provided into space, time, and gravity, fundamentally altered the way we view the cosmos. It was not the number of theories that made Einstein great, but the depth and power of his insights. In a world where individuals often chase quantity, striving to produce more, Einstein's legacy teaches us that true greatness often resides in the quality of one's ideas. The impact of his theory continues to resonate in fields ranging from quantum mechanics to space exploration. Einstein's life reminds us that the value of a singular, profound achievement far exceeds the merit of numerous trivial accomplishments.

"One good act is worth a thousand lesser deeds."

Chapter 2

Knowledge and Wisdom

Knowledge is the accumulation of facts, but wisdom is the ability to use them rightly. While knowledge informs, wisdom transforms. A mind full of information may still lack understanding, but a wise mind sees beyond facts, drawing meaningful connections. Knowledge is acquired through study, but wisdom is cultivated through experience and reflection. It is not about how much one knows but how well one applies what is known. True wisdom embraces humility, knowing that learning never ends. A wise person listens, observes, and grows, realizing that understanding is far greater than mere intelligence. History distinguishes between mere knowledge and true wisdom. The Renaissance sparked an age of learning, but wisdom lies in applying knowledge ethically. Figures like Aristotle and Buddha exemplify that wisdom comes from experience, reflection, and the pursuit of truth beyond facts.

In wealth, he's blind to his riches' gleam.
In poverty, generosity's a fleeting dream.
Balance lies in neither extreme,
But in wisdom's steady, tempered beam.

Balance in Life

The poem reveals the pitfalls of living at extremes—wealth often blinds people to gratitude and generosity, while poverty can foster bitterness and despair. True happiness and fulfillment lie in a balanced perspective, where neither riches nor deprivation dictate actions. It advocates for temperance, with wisdom as the guiding light. Those who find balance appreciate life's blessings without attachment and give freely without resentment. Life's true wealth is measured not by material possessions but by the richness of spirit and thoughtfulness of action. Striking this balance is key to leading a meaningful life.

A rich merchant boasted about his wealth, ignoring his family, while a poor farmer worked tirelessly, always lamenting his misfortune. A wise sage visited both and gave them a challenge—to carry a bowl of water without spilling a drop while walking a path of treasures and pitfalls. The merchant spilled his water, distracted by the treasures, and the farmer, overwhelmed by obstacles, did the same. The sage taught, "Balance lies in focusing on what matters." Both men changed—appreciating their blessings and giving more to others, finding contentment in harmony.

Andrew Carnegie, one of the richest men of his time, could have lived a life of luxury and indulgence. Instead, he chose to invest his fortune in people. Carnegie funded libraries, schools, and cultural institutions, believing that true wealth lay in the ability to enrich the lives of others. His philanthropy provided opportunities for education and growth, especially for the underprivileged.

Carnegie's story is a powerful reminder that life's true richness isn't measured in dollars or possessions. It's found in the connections we build, the knowledge we share, and the lives we uplift. His legacy teaches us to see wealth not as an end but as a means to create a better world. In giving, we find a richness that materialism can never provide.

"Moderation is the key to happiness."

After sipping nectar, who craves milk's stream?
Realizing truth, beauty fades from esteem.
Life's essence surpasses a fleeting dream,
Illuminating the eternal in its gleam.

The Essence of Truth

Once one experiences the nectar of truth, superficial pleasures lose their charm. Beauty and material allure pale in comparison to the profound satisfaction of realizing life's true essence. The poem emphasizes the eternal over the fleeting, urging us to seek deeper meaning and purpose. Truth provides clarity and fulfillment, surpassing transient dreams. Life's real value lies in recognizing and embracing the eternal truths that illuminate existence. It calls us to transcend the mundane and focus on what holds lasting significance, elevating our perception of life and its meaning.

A prince indulged in luxury until he met a wandering monk who spoke of inner peace. Intrigued, the prince joined him in meditation, experiencing a serenity he had never known. Returning to his palace, the prince found his former pleasures hollow. Inspired, he used his wealth to help others, discovering that true joy lay in the simplicity of serving and understanding life's essence.

At 15, Malala Yousafzai was shot by the Taliban for advocating girls' education. Instead of silencing her, the attack amplified her voice. Malala continued her fight for education, becoming a global icon for equality and winning the Nobel Peace Prize. Her courage inspired millions, proving that truth and justice outweigh fear and oppression.

Malala's story is a powerful reminder that higher truths—equality, education, and justice—transcend the temporary victories of fear. Her journey encourages us to stand firm in our beliefs, knowing that one voice can spark a global movement.

"Truth is eternal."

Science without self-experience is frail.
A picture of light won't make darkness pale.
Truth comes from deeds, not a fabricated tale,
For wisdom blooms in life's honest trail.

The Depth of True Understanding

Science and knowledge are meaningful only when grounded in experience and action. A mere image of light cannot eliminate darkness, just as superficial knowledge cannot replace the wisdom gained through genuine effort. The poem highlights the importance of deeds over empty words, emphasizing that truth and understanding emerge from living an authentic and honest life. Knowledge without self-application is shallow and ineffective. It calls us to pursue wisdom through practice and real-life engagement, rejecting superficiality in favor of depth and authenticity.

A professor lectured on the science of fire to his students but had never kindled one himself. A farmer overhearing said, "Come, light my stove." Struggling, the professor failed, while the farmer easily lit it. Embarrassed, the professor realized that knowledge without application is hollow. From that day, he blended theory with practice, teaching students the importance of real-world experience. His revised approach transformed not only his lessons but also his students, who became better prepared for life.

The Wright Brothers, Orville and Wilbur, were bicycle mechanics with a dream: human flight. While many scientists and engineers theorized about the mechanics of flying, the

Wright brothers took a different approach. They built and tested gliders, learning from each experiment. By observing birds and refining their designs through trial and error, they gained insights that no amount of theoretical study could offer.

On December 17, 1903, their hard work paid off. Their airplane, the Flyer, made the first sustained, powered flight in Kitty Hawk, North Carolina. It lasted just 12 seconds but proved that humanity could conquer the skies.

The Wright brothers' story is a testament to the power of practical experience. While theory lays the foundation, it is experience that brings dreams to life. Their journey reminds us that success often requires stepping beyond books and taking risks in the real world.

"Experience is the best teacher."

One may master science, high and low,
Yet life's ultimate truth they'll never know.
What's learning worth if death's secrets don't show?
For wisdom deepens when the soul does grow.

Wisdom Beyond Knowledge

This poem reflects on the limits of intellectual knowledge when it does not address life's ultimate truth. Mastering science and learning all things in the material world may provide knowledge, but it cannot uncover the profound mysteries of life, death, and the soul. True wisdom arises not from external education but from spiritual growth and self-awareness. Only when the soul evolves does wisdom deepen, revealing truths beyond what can be understood through intellect alone.

A great scholar spent years studying science and philosophy, seeking to master every subject. He was praised for his knowledge and intellect. Yet, despite his vast learning, he found himself fearful of death, unable to comprehend its meaning. One day, he met an elderly man who had never studied in books but lived a simple life full of compassion. The old man spoke of life's mysteries, not through intellectual reasoning but through deep spiritual wisdom. The scholar realized that no amount of learning could prepare him for the truth of life and death. True wisdom, he understood, comes from within the soul, not from external sources.

Knowledge Without Purpose

Education is often perceived as the accumulation of knowledge—mastering subjects, excelling in science, and acquiring technical skills. However, true education goes beyond intellectual pursuits; it is a journey of self-discovery and inner growth. The statement, "Education is the manifestation of perfection already in man," beautifully aligns with the wisdom in the poem, which questions the value of learning if it does not lead to a deeper understanding of life's ultimate truth.

One may gain expertise in science, exploring the mysteries of the universe, yet remain unaware of the deeper realities of existence. If learning does not illuminate the path to self-awareness and wisdom, it remains incomplete. True education does not merely inform but transforms, helping individuals realize their innate potential and guiding them toward spiritual and moral enlightenment. It is not just about seeking answers in books but about introspection and personal growth.

Real wisdom comes when education nurtures both the intellect and the soul. When learning fosters compassion, integrity, and an understanding of life's deeper purpose, it becomes meaningful. The highest form of education is not about conquering the external world but about mastering oneself. Only when knowledge is accompanied by self-awareness does it truly lead to enlightenment, revealing the perfection that has always existed within.

Socrates, the ancient Greek philosopher, is renowned for his teachings that challenged conventional wisdom and sought to uncover deeper truths about life and existence. One of his central ideas was that knowledge without purpose is ultimately meaningless. Socrates believed that acquiring knowledge for knowledge's sake was a shallow pursuit. True wisdom, in his view, comes not from accumulating facts, but from seeking to understand life's deeper meaning. His teachings encouraged his students to question everything, particularly the nature of mortality, virtue, and purpose. Socrates himself famously claimed that "the unexamined life is not worth living," emphasizing the importance of introspection and self-awareness in the pursuit of knowledge. He urged his followers to understand not just the world around them, but their own inner nature. Socrates' philosophy resonates today, reminding us that knowledge is most valuable when it is used to improve the self and contribute to the greater good. His ideas also challenge us to consider whether our own knowledge is aligned with our deeper values, and to question whether we are seeking true understanding or merely accumulating facts without purpose.

"The more I learn, the more I realize how much I don't know."

Truth and wisdom, hand in hand,
Together, they make a scholar stand.
Virtue's mark is this noble brand,
For knowledge alone cannot command.

The Union of Truth and Wisdom

Truth and wisdom are inseparable. Wisdom needs the foundation of truth to be genuine and effective. A scholar who possesses wisdom but not truth may possess knowledge but lacks the moral and ethical grounding necessary for true understanding. Virtue, symbolized as the "noble brand," marks those who have not only accumulated knowledge but also lived following it. Knowledge alone is insufficient to make someone wise; it must be accompanied by an understanding of truth and virtue. Wisdom, when guided by truth, becomes a powerful force for good. True scholars are those who not only study but also embody the values of honesty, integrity, and virtue, creating a harmonious balance between intellect and morality. This combination is what makes a person truly wise.

In a small village, a teacher was known for his vast knowledge but lacked humility. One day, he was asked by a student, "What is more important—knowledge or wisdom?" The teacher arrogantly replied, "Knowledge, of course!" The student then said, "But isn't wisdom the ability to apply knowledge correctly, with integrity and truth?" The teacher realized that while he had gathered much knowledge, he lacked the wisdom to use it for the good of others. From then on, he dedicated himself to not only acquiring knowledge but also practicing truth and virtue in every aspect of his life.

Interconnection of Truth and Wisdom

Albert Einstein, one of the greatest minds in human history, revolutionized our understanding of the universe through his theory of relativity. Yet, Einstein's genius was not just in the mathematical and scientific truths he uncovered, but in the profound wisdom that came with it. His theories on space, time, and energy challenged existing paradigms and opened up new ways of thinking about the cosmos. However, Einstein's intellectual greatness extended beyond his contributions to science. He understood that truth is not just a collection of facts, but a deeper wisdom that connects human beings to the universe and to one another. His insights into relativity were not mere technical achievements; they embodied a more holistic understanding of the interconnection of all things in existence. Einstein's work illustrated the delicate balance between truth and wisdom, demonstrating how intellectual breakthroughs are often tied to a deeper, philosophical understanding of life. His wisdom was also evident in his social and political stances, where he used his platform to advocate for peace, civil rights, and social justice. Einstein's legacy shows that true greatness lies in the harmony between understanding the factual world and embracing the wisdom that guides us through it.

"Knowledge is power, but wisdom is its application."

Sour mangoes ripen into sweet,
As wisdom matures through learning's feat.
The wise know time's steady beat,
For patience reveals what haste won't meet.

Wisdom Matures with Time

Just as a mango ripens over time from sour to sweet, wisdom also matures through learning, experience, and patience. It cannot be rushed or forced. Wisdom takes time to develop and requires the calm reflection that only comes with age and experience. Hastiness leads to mistakes, but with time, the lessons learned through life's challenges reveal themselves in a deeper, more meaningful way. Those who are patient, who wait for wisdom to reveal itself, will eventually understand what those who rush will never comprehend.

A young man named Prem was eager to become the wisest person in his village. He studied diligently, read many books, and attended every lecture he could find. But despite his vast knowledge, he still lacked wisdom. One day, he met an old sage who had lived through many experiences. The sage asked Prem to stop rushing and reflect on his actions. "Wisdom is not a product of learning alone," the sage said. "It is the ability to understand life's complexities and its timing." Prem began to slow down, and over the years, he found that wisdom came not from knowledge alone, but from experiencing life and learning from it. In time, his reputation as the wisest man in the village was earned—not from books, but from patience and reflection.

Wisdom of Maturity

Mahatma Gandhi's life is a profound example of the wisdom that comes with maturity and the transformation that can occur over time. Gandhi, who began his career as a timid lawyer in South Africa, gradually evolved into one of the most influential leaders in the world. His journey was marked by deep personal introspection, struggles, and a growing understanding of the power of non-violence. In his early years, Gandhi was unsure of himself and uncertain of his path, but as he matured, his character became defined by a deep sense of justice, compassion, and wisdom. His commitment to truth and nonviolent resistance was not an inherent trait but developed through years of personal growth and spiritual practice. Gandhi's transformation exemplifies how wisdom is often born from patience, experience, and learning from life's challenges. His leadership in the Indian independence movement was characterized by calm resolve and a deep understanding of human nature, demonstrating that true greatness is often achieved through the passage of time and the refinement of one's character. Gandhi's life is a testament to the fact that wisdom, patience, and sweetness are cultivated over time, and maturity brings a deeper understanding of the world and its people.

"Patience is the key to wisdom."

The washerman's wisdom outweighs the elite,
A loyal dog's love is a pious feat,
And truth outshines a ruler's deceit,
For humility holds strength, pure and sweet.

Humility and Truth's Unshakable Power

Humility and truth possess greater power than wealth or high status. A washerman, despite being of humble means, can possess wisdom that surpasses the elite. A dog's loyalty holds greater value than any material possession, and truth shines brighter than any ruler's deceit. True strength lies not in pride or deceit, but in humility and authenticity. These virtues hold a timeless power that outlasts all other pursuits.

A powerful king once gathered his advisors and asked them, "What is the most valuable thing in life?" One advisor, dressed in royal attire, answered, "Gold and wealth are the keys to power." Another suggested, "Strength and force will bring dominance." But a humble washerman, standing in the back, said, "Truth and humility are the greatest virtues. Even the poorest man with a kind heart holds more value than a kingdom built on lies." The king, moved by the words, realized that true greatness comes from within, not from external power or possessions.

True Wisdom and Reality

The Wright brothers, Orville and Wilbur Wright, exemplified true wisdom by blending practical knowledge with persistence. In a world where many believed human flight was impossible, the Wright brothers focused not on theoretical ideas but on experimentation and hands-on learning. Their understanding of aerodynamics, engineering, and mechanics was grounded in reality—unlike other inventors of their time, who relied too heavily on abstract concepts. Their success in creating the first powered, controlled flight in 1903 demonstrated the immense value of real-world wisdom. The Wright brothers faced numerous setbacks and failures, but their determination and willingness to learn from mistakes kept them moving forward. Their achievement was not just the result of theoretical knowledge but of rigorous testing, failure, and refinement. They recognized that true wisdom is not merely knowing the answers but understanding the complexities of the real world and adapting to them. Their story is a reminder that practical experience often outweighs theoretical knowledge, and that perseverance, grounded in understanding reality, is the key to achieving remarkable feats.

"Humility is the foundation of true strength."

Speak not your secrets to a fool,
For he will break your trust's rule.
The village will know; you'll feel the duel,
For wisdom is guarded, not played as a tool.

The Dangers of Confiding in Fools

Confiding in a fool can lead to betrayal and harm. A fool does not understand the value of trust and is likely to spread your secrets or use them against you. Wisdom, on the other hand, knows the importance of discretion and the careful guarding of knowledge. Speaking your secrets to someone who lacks wisdom is akin to handing over a weapon to an enemy. The key to trust lies in sharing your inner thoughts only with those who have earned it.

A king, feeling troubled, sought advice from a trusted advisor. He shared his worries and secrets, hoping to find guidance. However, the advisor was a fool, unable to keep the king's trust. Soon, the entire kingdom knew of the king's private matters. His enemies used the information to plot against him. The king, ashamed, learned that trust should never be given to those unworthy of it. He vowed to only confide in wise and loyal individuals, understanding that trust is a sacred bond, not to be broken by the foolish.

Guarding Secrets

Edward Snowden's revelations about the National Security Agency's (NSA) surveillance programs in 2013 exposed the dark side of government secrets and their far-reaching consequences. Snowden, a former NSA contractor, leaked classified documents that revealed the scope of the U.S. government's mass surveillance on citizens, sparking global debates about privacy, security, and civil liberties. While some saw Snowden as a whistleblower and hero for exposing government overreach, others viewed him as a traitor who endangered national security. Snowden's actions underscore the complex relationship between the need for secrecy and the public's right to know. His revelations caused a profound shift in the way governments and individuals view privacy, with increased awareness of how information can be controlled and manipulated. Snowden's story serves as a reminder of the power of secrets and the responsibility that comes with possessing sensitive information. It also emphasizes the importance of discretion and the potential dangers of disclosing secrets without fully considering the consequences. His actions left a lasting impact on global politics and the debate surrounding privacy rights, illustrating how one individual's decision to reveal hidden truths can reshape societal norms.

"Trust the wise with your secrets, not the fool, for they will turn them into weapons."

Chapter 3

Unity and Strength

Strength does not come from numbers alone but from a shared purpose. When individuals stand together with trust and cooperation, they create an unbreakable force. Unity fosters resilience, allowing people to overcome obstacles that seem impossible alone. Division weakens and leads to downfall, but unity builds harmony and progress. True strength is not about overpowering others but about supporting one another. Whether in families, communities, or societies, unity breeds success, while discord leads to failure. In the end, strength is not measured by force but by the ability to stand together despite differences. Whether the Roman Empire's discipline or India's freedom struggle thrived on unity. Disunity, on the other hand, has led to the downfall of mighty empires.

The blind and lame cannot part ways,
Together they tread through life's maze.
So the poor find strength in shared days,
For unity brings light through darkened haze.

Strength in Unity

Individuals with limitations can overcome challenges through cooperation. A blind person and a lame one, though weak alone, complement each other's strengths, navigating life's difficulties together. Similarly, those with little can achieve much by working in unity. Collective effort is a powerful tool for overcoming adversity and that strength lies in mutual support. By fostering collaboration and harmony, even the most daunting challenges can be surmounted, teaching us the value of interdependence and shared purpose.

In a drought-stricken village, two struggling farmers decided to pool their resources—one had seeds but no water, and the other had water but no seeds. Together, they planted crops and shared the harvest, surviving the hardship. Inspired by their success, the entire village united to solve their water crisis, building a reservoir through collective effort. Their unity transformed despair into abundance, proving that collaboration can overcome even the direst circumstances.

In 1948, the Soviet Union imposed a blockade on West Berlin, cutting off food, fuel, and essential supplies in an attempt to force the Allies out of the city. Faced with a humanitarian crisis, the United States, Britain, and other Allied nations launched the Berlin Airlift—a monumental effort to deliver supplies by air.

For nearly a year, planes flew day and night, landing every few minutes, delivering everything from coal to chocolate. Over 3 million tons of supplies were delivered, sustaining the isolated city. This extraordinary effort, achieved through unity and collaboration, eventually forced the Soviets to lift the blockade in 1949.

The Berlin Airlift is a shining example of how unity can overcome adversity. It proved that when people come together for a common cause, even seemingly insurmountable challenges can be conquered. This story inspires us to find strength in solidarity and to stand together in the face of difficulty.

Unity Amid Adversity

The Underground Railroad was a beacon of hope for enslaved people in the 19th-century United States. This covert network, comprising abolitionists, both Black and white, risked their lives to guide individuals to freedom in the North. It wasn't a literal railroad but a series of safe houses and secret routes.

Harriet Tubman, one of its most famous conductors, escaped slavery herself and returned multiple times to guide others to freedom. Her courage and the collective effort of countless unsung heroes saved thousands from bondage. Despite facing brutal opposition, they worked together, driven by the shared belief in freedom and humanity.

The Underground Railroad is a testament to the strength of unity in adversity. It shows that when people come together for a just cause, they can challenge even the darkest injustices. This story inspires us to stand united and fight for what is right, no matter the odds.

"Unity is strength."

The beasts' colors differ, but milk is the same,
Flowers are diverse, yet prayers acclaim.
Our views vary, but God holds no blame,
For His essence transcends our earthly name.

Unity Beyond Diversity

While the outward forms of life are diverse—beasts with different colors, and flowers with various hues—there is an underlying unity in the essential aspects of life. Milk is the same regardless of the animal, and prayers seek the same divine essence regardless of the words or rituals. Similarly, humans may have different perspectives, but God's essence transcends all these differences. Beyond every outward diversity, there lies a common spiritual truth, encouraging tolerance, unity, and reverence for the divine in all forms.

In a village, people from different cultures gathered for a feast. They spoke different languages, wore different clothes, and practiced different traditions. But when the elders began singing prayers in unison, all felt a deep connection, transcending their differences. A young traveler, witnessing this, asked an elder why they all prayed the same way. The elder replied, "While we may walk different paths, we all seek the same light." From that day, the traveler spread the message of unity and shared purpose, realizing that, despite our differences, we all share a common divine connection.

The Harlem Globetrotters, a basketball team of extraordinary talent, rose to fame not just for their skills but for their message of unity. Formed during an era of racial segregation in the United States, the team brought together players of different races and backgrounds, showcasing the beauty of diversity on and off the court.

Their entertaining style, blending athleticism with humor, drew massive audiences and broke racial barriers. During the Civil Rights Movement, the Globetrotters became ambassadors of goodwill, proving that passion and talent transcend prejudice. Their global tours fostered understanding and inspired social change.

The Globetrotters remind us that unity in diversity isn't just a concept—it's a powerful force that can heal divisions and inspire progress. Their story highlights the strength of embracing differences to create something extraordinary.

"Diversity is the one true thing we all have in common."

Trustworthy men deserve your care,
Avoid mingling with the wealthy's snare.
Poverty opens accounts none can bear,
But integrity remains beyond compare.

Integrity Over Wealth

While wealth may provide temporary comfort, it cannot buy true value or happiness. Wealthy individuals are often respected for their material possessions, but integrity is the true measure of a person's worth. Trustworthiness, honesty, and moral strength are priceless qualities that cannot be bought or sold. Those who possess these virtues are far more valuable than any rich man, for integrity remains untarnished by the fluctuations of fortune, while wealth can vanish in an instant.

A young merchant named Arun was offered a lucrative deal by a wealthy businessman who was known for his dishonest practices.

Despite the financial gains, Arun was uncomfortable with the idea of working with someone whose integrity he doubted. He decided to partner with a humble and trustworthy man, despite knowing that the financial rewards would be much smaller. Over time, Arun's business prospered through honest hard work, and his reputation for integrity grew. Meanwhile, the wealthy businessman faced legal troubles and lost everything, including his respect. Arun realized that wealth could come and go, but integrity was something that would last forever.

Pranks and Caution

The Dot-com Bubble of the late 1990s offers a cautionary tale about the dangers of reckless optimism and imprudent behavior in the financial world. During this period, the rapid growth of the internet led to a surge in investments in internet-based companies. However, many investors did not exercise due diligence or thoroughly evaluate the sustainability of these companies, assuming that all tech companies would succeed simply because of their connection to the internet. This irrational exuberance led to the creation of an economic bubble, where companies were overvalued, and their stock prices inflated beyond reasonable expectations. When the bubble burst in 2000, millions of investors faced massive financial losses. The collapse caused ripple effects throughout the economy, with many companies going bankrupt, and thousands of people losing jobs. The Dot-com Bubble teaches the importance of caution in financial decision-making. Blind speculation without a solid understanding of the market and the true value of investments can lead to disastrous consequences. This event serves as a reminder that what may initially seem like harmless pranks or easy opportunities in business can quickly turn into cautionary lessons when reckless decisions are made.

"Integrity is worth more than gold."

Mean minds fail to see God's unity,
Anger distorts magical acuity.
Wisdom rises above such disparity,
For peace embraces life's clarity.

The Distortion of Anger and the Clarity of Peace

Anger clouds judgment and distorts the mind's clarity, leading to poor decisions and a lack of understanding. Those who fail to see the unity of life, due to their anger or ignorance, are unable to experience true wisdom. Peace, on the other hand, clears the mind and allows for deeper understanding. A calm and peaceful heart fosters wisdom, while anger leads to confusion and misunderstanding. Wisdom and clarity come from a peaceful mind, which embraces the interconnectedness of all things.

In a kingdom, there was a wise sage known for his calm demeanor. One day, a young man came to him, furious about a wrong he had suffered. "The world is unfair!" the young man shouted. "I must seek vengeance!" The sage replied, "Anger clouds the mind. It will distort the clarity you need to understand the truth of your situation." The young man was skeptical, but as he sat with the sage and calmed his emotions, he began to see the situation from a different perspective. "Peace is the key to wisdom," he said, grateful for the sage's guidance. He learned that anger had only obscured his ability to see the truth.

Unity Beyond Differences

Mother Teresa, known for her selfless work with the poor and sick in Calcutta (now Kolkata), embodied the wisdom of seeing beyond divisions to recognize the inherent unity of humanity. She devoted her life to serving those who were marginalized and ignored by society, regardless of their religion, nationality, or social status. Whether caring for the sick, the homeless, or those dying in the streets, Mother Teresa saw the divinity in every person she helped, recognizing that we are all part of one human family. Her approach was rooted in compassion and love, demonstrating that true service comes from a place of deep respect for others as fellow human beings. Mother Teresa's work transcended societal divisions, showing that unity lies in our shared humanity. By focusing on the needs of others without considering differences, she reminded the world that we are all interconnected, and that each person, regardless of their background or circumstances, deserves dignity, respect, and love. Her life is a powerful example of the transformative power of seeing beyond superficial differences and embracing the unity of humanity, grounded in the belief that we are all children of the same divine source.

"Anger is a short madness; peace is the gateway to wisdom."

Chapter 4

Human Nature and Behavior

Human nature is a blend of emotions, desires, and reasoning. At times, people act with kindness and compassion, while at other times, they are driven by selfish motives. Behavior is shaped by circumstances, experiences, and personal values. While some respond to challenges with patience and wisdom, others react impulsively, leading to regret. Understanding human nature helps in fostering better relationships and decision-making. It is neither entirely good nor bad but constantly evolving. The key lies in self-awareness and conscious choices, which determine whether one nurtures positive qualities or falls into patterns of negativity. From Machiavelli's political realism to Rousseau's belief in innate goodness, history debates human nature. Wars, revolutions, and acts of compassion reveal the complexities of human behavior, proving that circumstances shape actions, but moral choices define humanity.

The boastful prattle, hollow and loud,
Contrasts the sage, gentle and proud.
Gold never clinks like cheap metal allowed,
Its quiet shine humbles the ostentatious crowd.

Quiet Wisdom

True greatness doesn't announce itself loudly. Gold, though valuable, doesn't clink like cheaper metals. The boastful often mask their insecurities with noise, while the wise let their actions speak softly yet profoundly. This poem contrasts ostentation with genuine worth, reminding us that quiet dignity holds more weight than loud self-promotion. A wise person values substance over show and earns respect through deeds rather than words. Just as gold's quiet shine outlasts the clamor of tin, true wisdom humbles rather than exalts, leaving a lasting impression on those around.

A young man bragged loudly about his achievements, seeking attention. An elder, silently helping others, earned admiration without a word. When the young man asked why no one praised him, the elder said, "True worth shines without noise." Humbled, the young man learned the value of quiet wisdom.

In the 1858 Illinois Senate debates, Abraham Lincoln faced Stephen Douglas, a fiery and charismatic speaker. While Douglas relied on his loud, aggressive rhetoric, Lincoln remained calm and composed. He spoke with measured words, letting logic and reason guide his arguments. His gentle yet firm demeanor won the hearts of the audience, proving that strength lies not in the volume of speech but in its substance.

Lincoln's story teaches us that true leadership isn't about dominating a room but about inspiring trust and respect. Just as gold's soft glow surpasses the clanging of lesser metals, quiet dignity often leaves a lasting impression. Lincoln's debates remind us to speak with purpose and listen with understanding, for it is gentle wisdom, not loud boasts, that truly moves hearts.

"Empty vessels make the most noise."

A son without care for his kin,
Is worthless, in life or deep within.
Like termites, their existence is thin,
Devouring bonds, leaving ruin akin.

Merciless Children

A son who neglects his family's love and bonds brings no value to himself or others. Such disregard, like termites, weakens the very foundation of relationships, leaving nothing but destruction. One must know the importance of loyalty, care, and respect within a family. A strong family bond provides strength and stability, while its absence leads to isolation and emptiness. It warns that selfishness erodes these connections, leaving behind ruins instead of unity. Nurturing kinship is a vital part of a meaningful life.

A wealthy merchant disowned his aging parents, prioritizing wealth over family. Years later, his son abandoned him in his old age. Alone and regretful, the merchant visited his parents, seeking forgiveness. His parents, despite the neglect, welcomed him back with open arms, teaching him the value of unconditional love. Realizing his folly, the merchant reconciled with his family and devoted himself to strengthening their bond, ensuring his son learned the value of respect and care.

During Pol Pot's brutal Khmer Rouge regime in Cambodia, children became both victims and perpetrators. The regime indoctrinated young minds, turning them into tools of oppression. These children, devoid of empathy, carried out unimaginable atrocities, including executions of their elders and peers.

This dark chapter in history highlights the peril of corrupting youth with misplaced ideology. Innocence turned merciless under the weight of manipulation. Pol Pot's regime warns us of the devastating consequences when the purity of youth is twisted by hatred. It's a call to nurture compassion and critical thinking in future generations.

"A family in harmony prospers in everything."

A boulder can be shattered with force.
Hills may crumble, yielding to the course.
But the hard-hearted stand with no remorse,
Immovable, they resist truth's force.

The Unyielding Heart

A boulder can be shattered, and hills may erode, but a hardened heart resists even the mightiest forces. The poem reflects on the stubbornness and lack of empathy in those who refuse to embrace truth or compassion. Unlike physical obstacles that yield to pressure, the unyielding heart remains immovable, obstructing growth and understanding. It warns against the dangers of insensitivity and rigidity, urging us to cultivate openness and compassion. A flexible mind and a kind heart pave the way for harmony and progress, while obstinacy leads to isolation and stagnation.

A kind sage approached a tyrant king, urging him to show mercy to his oppressed people. The king, unmoved, ignored the sage's advice. Years later, a rebellion dethroned the king, who fled to the same sage for refuge. The sage remarked, "A boulder that refuses to bend will eventually crumble." Realizing his mistake, the king vowed to rule with compassion if given another chance. Restored to the throne, he became a beloved ruler, learning that humility and empathy lead to lasting strength.

During the Spanish Inquisition, rigid dogma often silenced progress and innovation. Galileo Galilei, one of history's greatest scientific minds, faced persecution for supporting heliocentrism—the idea that the Earth orbits the Sun. Despite presenting clear evidence, the Inquisition forced Galileo to recant his findings, prioritizing dogmatic beliefs over truth.

This period of history illustrates the dangers of inflexible thinking. Unyielding hearts stifle progress, clinging to outdated ideas even when faced with overwhelming evidence. Galileo's story, however, also serves as a beacon of resilience. Although silenced in his time, his ideas eventually reshaped humanity's understanding of the universe.

This tale reminds us to embrace open-mindedness and courage. Progress often comes from challenging established norms, and truth, though suppressed, will always find its way into the light.

"A stubborn heart invites its own downfall."

A dog at a palace won't turn into a lion,
A pig at a temple won't match an elephant's horizon.
An unlearned man stays so, no matter the region,
For wisdom's light cannot be blinded by legion.

Wisdom is Beyond Status

No matter where one is placed or what surroundings they find themselves in, their true potential for wisdom cannot be altered by external circumstances. A dog, no matter how it is positioned, will never become a lion, just as an unlearned person cannot acquire wisdom simply by being in learned circles. True wisdom is not dependent on status, wealth, or surroundings but on one's inner pursuit of knowledge and understanding. Wisdom is an internal quality that cannot be masked by external appearances or environments.

A young man from a poor village was often ridiculed for his lack of education, while his wealthy peers boasted of their learning. One day, an old scholar told him, "Knowledge doesn't depend on wealth or status. It's in the heart and mind." The young man began studying diligently, learning from nature, people, and life itself. Years later, he became renowned for his wisdom. He returned to his peers, not with riches, but with profound knowledge, proving that true wisdom cannot be bound by circumstance.

The fable of the scorpion and the frog tells the story of a scorpion asking a frog to carry him across a river. The frog hesitates, fearing the scorpion will sting him, but the scorpion promises not to. Halfway across the river, the scorpion stings the frog, sealing both of their fates. When the frog asks why, the scorpion replies, "It is in my nature."

This fable reflects a deep truth about human nature: despite promises or circumstances, inherent traits often define behavior. People can fall into destructive patterns even when they intend to change. The scorpion's instinct to sting mirrors how some individuals continue harmful actions despite knowing the consequences.

This story serves as a reminder that personal growth requires conscious effort, and the past cannot always be erased by promises alone. To overcome our inherent tendencies, we must actively change our thought patterns and behaviors, cultivating virtues rather than simply hoping for transformation.

"Wisdom does not wear a crown."

Scrubbing a rat won't make it white,
Nor will a wooden idol speak despite a fight.
Some things resist change, be it wrong or right,
For the essence remains, hidden from sight.

Unchangeable Nature

Trying to change something's inherent nature is useless. Just as scrubbing a rat won't make it white, or a wooden idol won't speak despite forceful attempts, some things cannot be altered by external means. The essence of things—be it a person's nature or an object's properties—remains unchanged regardless of appearances or efforts. No matter how much effort is put into transforming something fundamentally, its true essence will remain hidden but intact.

A man found an old, weathered idol and tried to force it to speak. He scrubbed and polished it, hoping it would grant him wisdom. But no matter how hard he tried, the idol remained silent. One day, a wise elder told him, "No matter how much you polish a stone, it cannot sing like a bird." The man realized that some things are beyond change, and true wisdom lies not in forcing change but in accepting the natural course of life. He began seeking wisdom within, understanding that true transformation begins within.

Marie Antoinette, the queen of France during its financial crisis in the late 18th century, became infamous for her reputed response to the starving masses: "Let them eat cake." Whether or not she actually uttered these words, her apparent indifference to the plight of the poor symbolizes a failure to empathize and adapt to her circumstances.

Her inability to change her extravagant lifestyle during a time of national suffering contributed to the rising resentment that ultimately led to the French Revolution. The queen's unyielding nature and disregard for the common people's struggles marked the end of her reign and her life.

Marie Antoinette's story is a cautionary tale about the dangers of stubbornness and detachment from the reality of others' suffering. It reminds us that leadership requires empathy, adaptability, and a sense of responsibility to those we serve.

"Old habits die hard."

Mingling with the base brings despair,
Even the great face harm unaware.
Like drinking milk beneath a palm's glare,
For the shadows dim what was once fair.

The Dangers of Associating with the Wicked

One should be alert in associating with people who have a base or corrupt nature, as their influence can negatively affect even the greatest of individuals. The metaphor of drinking milk under the shadow of a palm tree mentioned in the poem suggests that what once seemed pure or good can become tainted in bad company. One's reputation and moral standing can be compromised by associating with those who are morally corrupt or unworthy of trust.

A great king, known for his wisdom, began to associate with a group of corrupt advisers. Over time, he noticed that his decisions, once revered, began to fail. His subjects grew disillusioned, and even his closest allies began to distance themselves. Seeking counsel from an elder, the king asked why his reign was faltering. The elder replied, "If you keep a sweet fruit in the middle of rotten ones, none can find its purity." Realizing his error, the king expelled the corrupt advisers and sought to surround himself with virtuous people. His reign flourished once again, and he learned the importance of choosing wise company.

Harmful Associations

The assassination of Julius Caesar on March 15, 44 BCE, is one of history's most infamous betrayals. Caesar, who had become the most powerful man in Rome, was murdered by a group of senators led by Brutus, a man he considered a friend and ally. Despite his political success, Caesar had made the fatal mistake of trusting the wrong people. Brutus, who was allegedly Caesar's illegitimate son, and other conspirators feared that Caesar's growing power would lead to the collapse of the Roman Republic and the establishment of a monarchy. In the end, Caesar's trust in those closest to him—many of whom he considered allies—led to his downfall. His assassination not only marked the end of the Roman Republic but also plunged Rome into a period of civil war, which ultimately led to the rise of the Roman Empire. The story of Caesar's betrayal illustrates the dangers of placing too much trust in those who might not have your best interests at heart. Despite his wisdom in many areas, Caesar's failure to recognize the treachery within his inner circle proved to be his undoing, teaching us that harmful associations can destroy even the most powerful leaders.

"A man is known by the company he keeps."

When the lion falls ill, even dogs jeer,
When weak, avoid stubbornness, my dear.
Adapt, for survival makes strength clear,
In humility, resilience will appear.

Adaptability and Humility

Only the man of wisdom knows the importance of adaptability and humility in times of weakness. If a lion falls ill, it will be jeered at by dogs. The lion knows when to keep quiet. When one is weak, stubbornness can lead to further harm. Instead, survival requires adaptability and a humble attitude. Strength is not always about standing firm; sometimes, it is about knowing when to adapt to changing circumstances and remaining humble in the face of adversity.

Once, a powerful lion fell ill and could no longer hunt. The other animals, once terrified of him, now jeered and mocked his weakness. The lion, too proud to ask for help, tried to fight off his illness but only grew weaker. One day, a wise owl spoke to the lion, saying, "True strength lies not in stubbornness but in humility and adaptability." The lion realized that by refusing to adapt, he had made his condition worse. He began to seek help from others and adjusted to his circumstances.

Eventually, he regained his strength, learning that humility and adaptability are key to survival.

Weakness and Vulnerability

Napoleon Bonaparte, once the Emperor of France and one of history's most celebrated military strategists, faced the harsh reality of vulnerability after his ultimate defeat at the Battle of Waterloo. Following his abdication, Napoleon was exiled to the remote island of Saint Helena, far from the European courts he had once dominated. In this isolated and humbling environment, Napoleon, who had once commanded armies and nations, was subjected to ridicule, betrayal, and a life of exile. The very men who had once been his allies now turned their backs on him, offering no loyalty or support. His exile was not just a physical punishment but a brutal reminder of his weakness and vulnerability. Despite his earlier greatness, Napoleon's fall from power illustrates how even the mightiest can be brought low in moments of weakness. It also highlights the fragility of human pride and the impermanence of fortune. Napoleon's downfall serves as a cautionary tale about the transient nature of power, and how quickly the tables can turn when one's strength wanes. In his final years, Napoleon was left to reflect on his past triumphs and failures, living out his last days in solitude, far removed from the grandeur he once knew.

"A wise man adapts himself to circumstances, as water shapes itself to the vessel that contains it."

Feed a neem tree milk for years,
Its bitter taste still reappears.
The mean can't turn generous through care,
For nature's core is never rare.

The Nature of the Mean

Feeding a neem tree milk for years cannot change its bitterness. No amount of external effort can change a person's true nature. The mean-spirited will remain so, no matter the kindness shown to them. A person's core nature cannot be altered by external gestures or care, as true transformation comes from within.

A generous man took in a miserly neighbor and tried to show him kindness. He gave him food, shelter, and even helped him with his work. After many years, the generous man expected that his kindness would change the neighbor's heart. However, the neighbor remained as selfish as ever. One day, the generous man asked, "Why haven't you changed? I have given you everything." The neighbor replied, "Your care may have nourished me physically, but my heart remains the same. Change must come from within, not from the outside." The man realized that no amount of external effort could change someone's fundamental nature.

Inherent Nature

Benedict Arnold, once a celebrated hero in the American Revolutionary War, is remembered not for his military achievements but for his notorious betrayal of his country.

Arnold was a talented general, respected by his peers for his bravery and strategic mind. However, his desire for personal glory and wealth led him to commit an act of treason against the very nation he had fought to create. Arnold secretly offered to surrender the fort at West Point to the British, a move that would have handed the critical post to the enemy. His motivations were driven by greed and a desire for recognition, both of which he felt were denied by the American Continental Congress. Arnold's nature, however, was one that could not be easily changed. Despite his outward success, his personal flaws—his ambition and thirst for power—ultimately led him down a path of betrayal. Like a neem tree that remains bitter regardless of its surroundings, Arnold's inherent nature could not be transformed, even by the grand ideals of the revolution. His actions are a cautionary tale about the consequences of allowing one's inner desires to overpower loyalty and integrity. Benedict Arnold's story serves as a reminder that one's fundamental character can often lead to downfall, no matter how accomplished or revered one may be.

"Once set in their ways, people rarely change."

One may heat a crooked stick to make it straight,
One may grind mighty hills to dust by fate,
But the hard-hearted remain in their state,
For change begins only when hearts await.

Change Begins in the Heart

This poem reflects on the transformative power of the heart and the limits of external efforts in changing one's character. While it is possible to manipulate physical objects, like heating a crooked stick to make it straight or grinding mighty hills into dust, the human heart cannot be easily changed by external forces. True transformation starts from within; it is not through force, manipulation, or external pressure that one's character is shaped, but through an open and willing heart. The "hard-hearted" are those who resist change, who are set in their ways and remain unyielding, no matter the circumstances. Real change, personal growth, and self-improvement only occur when the individual is ready and willing to embrace change. Only when hearts are open and willing to transform can true change take place. The process of growth, therefore, is an inner journey that requires patience and readiness.

A young man wanted to become wise, so he approached an elder and asked, "How can I change my life and become better?" The elder told him, "You cannot change a crooked tree with a straight stick or crush a mountain with your bare hands. Real change happens within." The young man was puzzled and asked, "But how can I change my heart?" The elder replied, "By opening it. The heart must be willing to change for true transformation to occur. When your heart is ready, the world around you will also change." The young man realized that no matter how hard he tried, unless he truly wanted to change from within, external efforts would be futile.

He spent the rest of his life nurturing kindness and humility in his heart.

Hard-Heartedness

The Berlin Wall, erected in 1961, became one of the most powerful symbols of division during the Cold War. This concrete barrier physically separated East and West Berlin, but its true significance lay in the ideological and political divisions it represented between communism and capitalism. For nearly three decades, the Wall stood as an unyielding barrier, both a physical structure and a metaphor for the harshness of political regimes. The hard-heartedness of the political forces that supported the Wall demonstrated an unwillingness to consider the humanity of those on either side. Families were separated, lives were destroyed, and the human spirit was crushed under the weight of political ideology. The Wall was a stark reminder of the lengths to which totalitarian regimes would go to enforce their will, showing that political divisions, when hardened by fear, can create barriers that are far more difficult to dissolve than even the most imposing physical structures. The eventual fall of the Wall in 1989 symbolized the triumph of unity and freedom, but it also revealed the profound damage caused by decades of ideological rigidity. The Berlin Wall stands as a testament to how hard-hearted political systems can harm the human soul, and how fragile political divisions can be once the spirit of reconciliation is allowed to thrive.

"Change begins with the heart."

A scorpion's poison tips its tail,
The snake's venom lies in its fangs.
But the wicked carry it without fail,
For their hearts, like poison, leave a trail.

The Poison of Wickedness

Like a scorpion or a snake that inherently carries poison, wicked people carry malice and deceit in their hearts. Their harmful nature is evident in their actions and words. No matter how much they try to mask their true nature, the poison within them will always come to the surface. The harm they cause is like a trail of destruction, affecting the lives of those around them. Wickedness is not easily concealed; it always finds a way to reveal itself, leaving others poisoned by its touch.

There was a man named Vikram who was known for his sharp tongue and his ability to deceive others. He enjoyed spreading rumors and creating conflicts for his own amusement. One day, he was invited to a village gathering where a wise elder shared a story about a serpent that could never change its poisonous nature. The elder said, "Like the serpent, those who carry poison within will never be able to change their essence." Vikram laughed it off, but soon after, he found himself isolated, as his toxic nature had driven away even his closest friends. He realized that just as a scorpion's poison could never be washed away, his deceitful ways had alienated him from everyone. Only then did he understand the elder's wisdom.

Poison in Wickedness

Adolf Hitler's role in World War II exemplifies the catastrophic power of wickedness in one individual. Fueled by extreme ideologies and a desire for control, Hitler's actions led to the deaths of millions of people, the destruction of entire countries, and the creation of a legacy of pain and suffering. His policies of racial superiority and hatred targeted Jews, disabled individuals, political opponents, and many others, culminating in the Holocaust—one of the darkest chapters of human history. Hitler's toxic ideology spread like poison, infecting his followers and inciting violence across Europe. The devastation he caused can be likened to a poison that permeates society, transforming ordinary men and women into perpetrators of unimaginable cruelty. His dictatorship highlighted the immense damage that a single person's wickedness can inflict upon the world. The aftermath of his reign serves as a reminder of the destructive power of evil, and how one individual's actions can unravel the fabric of civilization. The horrors of World War II and the Holocaust demonstrate that unchecked wickedness, when left to grow, can spread harm far and wide, leaving scars that may never fully heal.

"Those who spread venom will eventually drink it."

Words may be shaped without shame,
Stone may be carved, though wild it came.
But even the wise struggle with the mind's flame,
For thoughts are fickle, never the same.

The Struggle of the Mind and the Wisdom in Thought

Our thoughts are complex and ever-changing, just like a stone that can be carved into different shapes but remains rough and wild in its natural form. Even the wisest individuals struggle with controlling their minds, as thoughts are fickle and unpredictable. It is not easy to master one's mind, for it is constantly shifting. However, wisdom lies in understanding the nature of these fluctuations and learning to guide them toward clarity and purpose. Thoughts may wander, but true wisdom lies in shaping them toward meaningful action.

Once, a great king sought advice from a renowned sage who had mastered his mind and thoughts. "How do you keep your mind calm in times of crisis?" the king asked. The sage replied, "It's not about silencing your thoughts, but understanding them and guiding them toward peace. Even the wisest have fleeting, untamed thoughts. The trick is not to follow them blindly." The king, frustrated with his own restless mind, realized that controlling thoughts was not about perfection but about awareness and patience. Wisdom is not the absence of erratic thoughts but the ability to handle them with grace.

Control of the Mind

The Buddha's journey to enlightenment is one of the most powerful examples of the importance of controlling one's mind and attaining inner peace. Siddhartha Gautama, born a prince, had everything a person could desire, yet he sought something deeper: the meaning of suffering and the path to liberation. He renounced his royal life and embarked on a spiritual quest, encountering numerous teachings but ultimately discovering that true enlightenment came from within. Through meditation and mindfulness, the Buddha learned to master his thoughts, realizing that the mind is the source of all suffering and that control over one's mental state leads to freedom. The struggle to quiet the mind and attain peace is difficult for anyone, but the Buddha's teachings emphasize that it is possible through discipline, focus, and understanding. His journey from ignorance to enlightenment shows that mental mastery is not an easy path, but it is essential for achieving inner tranquility. The Buddha's teachings continue to resonate across cultures, reminding us of the importance of mastering our minds in a world often filled with distractions and turmoil. His life exemplifies that true peace comes from within, not from external circumstances.

"A wise man doesn't silence the mind; he learns to listen and understand."

A dog can't turn into a cow,
A rabbit a tiger—none knows how.
The miser's heart won't change, not now,
For nature's course is steadfast, and fixed is the vow.

The Immutable Nature of the Miser's Heart

Just as no animal can change its inherent nature—such as a dog cannot become a cow or a rabbit cannot transform into a tiger—similarly, a miser's heart remains unyielding. Despite external influences or experiences, the fundamental nature of a person, especially one driven by greed, is difficult to change. Nature's course is fixed, and people cannot easily alter their core instincts or characteristics. Therefore, we must understand that some qualities, like generosity or greed, are deeply ingrained and may resist transformation.

A young prince, full of hope, tried to change the heart of his miserly uncle, who hoarded wealth and refused to help the poor. The prince gave him gifts and attempted to show him the joy of sharing. Yet, no matter how hard he tried, the miser's heart remained unmoved. One day, the wise royal counselor told the prince, "A dog cannot become a cow, and a miser's heart will not change through mere gifts. Some natures are fixed, and we must learn to work with them, not fight them." The prince understood that some qualities are deeply rooted and that efforts to change them must be focused on finding balance, not forcing transformation.

The Hacker and the Startup Founder

In the bustling world of tech startups, Ryan had a dream—to build a revolutionary app that would change the way people managed their finances. After years of hard work, sleepless nights, and relentless determination, his startup, FinSync, was finally gaining traction. Investors were interested, users were signing up, and success seemed just within reach.

But there was one major problem—security. The app handled sensitive financial data, and Ryan knew that even the smallest breach could destroy his company overnight. He needed a cybersecurity expert, but hiring one was expensive, and time was running out.

One day, Ryan received an anonymous message:

"I know your system is vulnerable. I can help. No charge. No tricks. Just trust me."

The message was signed with a single name: "ZeroByte."

Ryan hesitated. ZeroByte was a well-known hacker, infamous for breaching major corporations. He had caused millions in damages, but oddly, he also claimed to expose flaws to make companies stronger. Some called him a cybercriminal; others saw him as a necessary evil.

Desperate, Ryan responded.

"If I let you in, can I trust you?"

"Of course," ZeroByte replied. "I live by a code: I never betray those who give me a chance."

Against his better judgment, Ryan granted ZeroByte access.

At first, it seemed like the right decision. The hacker strengthened the firewall, patched security holes, and even gave Ryan advice on how to defend against potential cyberattacks. Within weeks, FinSync was more secure than ever, and Ryan finally felt safe.

One evening, as Ryan relaxed with a cup of coffee, his phone buzzed. A notification flashed across the screen:

"Unauthorized Data Transfer Detected."

His heart pounded. He rushed to his laptop, only to see that FinSync's entire customer database—millions of names, bank details, and passwords—had been copied and wiped clean.

Panic set in. Investors started calling. Users were furious. The media ran headlines: "Massive Data Breach at FinSync—Trust Shattered!"

Ryan frantically messaged ZeroByte.

"Why?! You said I could trust you!"

A reply came almost instantly.

"I couldn't help it—it's in my nature."

And just like that, ZeroByte disappeared into the digital shadows, leaving Ryan to face the ruins of his once-promising startup.

"Some hearts weigh more in gold than in goodness."

Chapter 5

Wealth and Materialism

Wealth can provide comfort and security, but its pursuit without balance often leads to dissatisfaction. Material possessions may bring temporary pleasure, yet they do not guarantee happiness or fulfillment. True wealth lies in contentment, wisdom, and meaningful relationships. While financial stability is important, excessive attachment to materialism can lead to greed and restlessness. There is nothing wrong with seeking prosperity, but when wealth becomes the sole focus, it blinds one to the deeper joys of life. In the end, richness is not measured by what one owns but by the peace and purpose one carries within. Gold has toppled empires and fueled conquests, yet the pursuit of wealth often leads to moral decay. Figures like Emperor Ashoka and Marcus Aurelius realized that true prosperity lies in wisdom and contentment, not in material accumulation.

A single blue diamond outshines countless stones.
Why value numbers when only brilliance atones?
One poem can teach more than tomes of drones.
Quality surpasses the weight that quantity condones.

When Less Becomes Limitless

The True value lies in the brilliance and depth of quality, not in the abundance of quantity. A single, well-written poem has the power to inspire and teach more than an entire volume of mediocre works. A blue diamond, rare and unique, outshines countless ordinary stones. In life, focusing on depth, refinement, and meaning creates a lasting impact. Numbers can never replace excellence. Striving for quality elevates endeavors while chasing quantity often leads to superficiality. Whether in relationships, work, or achievements, it is the intrinsic worth that truly matters, not the weight or size of the collection.

A baker prided himself on producing the most bread in town, but his loaves were dry and tasteless. His competitor, though producing fewer loaves, crafted each with care, using the finest ingredients. Soon, customers flocked to the competitor, valuing the rich taste over abundance. The baker learned the importance of quality over quantity and started baking fewer but superior loaves. His business thrived once he prioritized excellence. This taught him that one masterpiece outweighs a thousand average creations.

The Teachings of Socrates

Socrates, the classical Greek philosopher, left no written records of his own. Compared to the vast volumes produced by others, he offered only spoken dialogues, preserved later by his students like Plato.

And yet—his few words and questions reshaped Western philosophy. His ideas on ethics, reasoning, and critical thinking became the foundation of countless schools of thought, influencing generations far more than libraries full of lesser-known texts.

"I know that I know nothing." — A single line from Socrates that challenged the world's understanding of knowledge itself.

When Socrates was brought to trial in Athens, accused of corrupting the youth and impiety, he stood before a jury of 500 citizens. Rather than pleading for his life, flattering the jury, or calling on influential allies (as many would have done), Socrates chose to speak the truth with courage and clarity.

He said: "I am not wise, but I know this: I do not know."

His defense was not long or elaborate, but his simple, sincere words challenged the hypocrisy of Athens. He compared himself to a gadfly, sent by the gods to sting the lazy horse of the Athenian state—provoking thought, not comfort.

Though he was sentenced to death, his few words inspired philosophical revolutions and moral inquiry for millennia.

"A diamond is precious, no matter how small."

The miser hoards without spending a part,
Neither for others nor his own heart.
Like the bee's hoard, looted as it departs,
Selfishness leaves an empty cart.

The Miser's Empty Legacy

A miser, in hoarding wealth without using it for himself or others, lives a hollow existence. Like a bee that gathers nectar only for it to be taken away, selfishness leaves nothing behind but emptiness. The poem warns against greed and self-centeredness, urging us to use our resources wisely and generously. Sharing wealth and joy enriches life and creates a meaningful legacy, while hoarding leads to isolation and regret. It encourages generosity as the antidote to selfishness, reminding us that what we give defines the impact we leave on the world.

A wealthy miser lived alone, hoarding gold but never spending it. When he passed away, his riches were discovered by thieves, leaving nothing for his family or community. Meanwhile, his poor neighbor, who shared what little he had, was mourned by the entire village for his kindness. Realizing the miser's wasted life, the villagers vowed to use their wealth for the greater good. The miser's unspent gold served as a stark reminder that generosity enriches the soul far more than hoarded treasures.

Hetty Green, known as the "Witch of Wall Street," was one of the wealthiest women of her time. Amassing a fortune equivalent to billions today, she was notorious for her extreme frugality. Despite her wealth, Hetty lived in cheap lodgings, wore tattered clothes, and refused to pay for medical care, even for her own son, whose untreated injury led to amputation.

Her life was a paradox of abundance and deprivation. While her financial acumen was remarkable, her inability to use her wealth for her benefit—or others'—rendered her life hollow. Her story became a cautionary tale of hoarding without purpose, a sharp contrast to philanthropists who use their fortunes to uplift society.

Hetty Green's life reminds us that wealth, hoarded and unused, becomes meaningless. True richness lies in using resources wisely, for personal fulfillment and the betterment of others.

"Wealth unused is wealth wasted."

The rich are praised like the moon's light,
The poor are lost in the world's sight.
Wealth defines who shines bright,
While true worth often remains out of sight.

The Illusion of Wealth and True Worth

The poem critiques the societal tendency to value wealth over character, suggesting that wealth, like the moon's light, is celebrated and admired, while the true worth of individuals often remains hidden in the shadows. Wealth is often equated with success, leaving the poor to be overlooked. However, true value is not always visible or measured in material possessions; it lies in one's character, actions, and integrity, which may not always receive the recognition they deserve in a world that idolizes outward appearances.

A wealthy merchant was celebrated by all for his fortune and lavish lifestyle. His servants, though kind-hearted and diligent, were barely noticed. One day, the merchant's wealth vanished in a series of bad investments. The servants, however, continued to serve him with loyalty and grace. The merchant, humbled by his loss, realized that it was the quiet virtue of his servants, not his own wealth, that had brought him peace and respect. He began to value them for their kindness and integrity, understanding that true worth lies in character, not in riches.

Andrew Carnegie, one of the wealthiest men in history, is often celebrated for his philanthropic efforts, particularly for funding over 2,500 public libraries. Yet, those who built these libraries—the laborers, construction workers, and artisans—remain largely unrecognized. Carnegie's wealth earned him public admiration, but the quiet efforts of those who made his vision a reality were left in the shadows.

This dichotomy reflects society's tendency to elevate those with wealth and power, while often neglecting the essential labor that supports success. Carnegie's generosity was significant, but it was built on the backs of countless individuals whose work was just as important. The story of Carnegie's libraries calls attention to the imbalance in how we value wealth over effort. It reminds us that recognition should extend beyond the elite, acknowledging the often invisible hands that contribute to success.

"Look beyond the surface before making a judgment."

To beg for wealth brings gods disgrace,
Friendship with fools invites dangers to face.
Pawned values reduce one's space,
For integrity is the heart's embrace.

The Consequences of Disgraceful Alliances

The poem warns against seeking wealth at the expense of integrity and caution in relationships. Begging for wealth brings disgrace, as does aligning oneself with those who lack wisdom, such as fools. It suggests that seeking material gain or companionship with those who do not share noble values can lead to ruin. True wealth and peace come from maintaining integrity and valuing meaningful relationships. It highlights that what is earned through virtue is far more valuable than what is gained through unscrupulous means.

A poor man, desperate for wealth, befriended a dishonest merchant known for his cunning ways. The merchant promised him riches, but the poor man, blinded by greed, ignored his better judgment. As time passed, the merchant's schemes caught up with him, and both were arrested. The poor man, now in prison, realized his mistake. He had forsaken his integrity for the promise of wealth, and in doing so, had lost everything. He vowed to never again trade his values for material gain. He learned that wealth built on virtue is far more precious than riches obtained through dishonest means.

Disgraceful Actions

Bernie Madoff's Ponzi scheme, one of the largest financial frauds in history, left thousands of investors devastated. Madoff's deceitful practices, which involved promising high returns to investors while using new funds to pay earlier investors, ultimately led to the collapse of his empire. His actions destroyed lives, shattered trust, and earned him widespread disgrace.

Madoff's downfall highlights the profound consequences of disgraceful behavior. What started as a manipulation of trust grew into a vast web of deceit, leaving devastation in its wake. Madoff's personal loss of dignity and the suffering he caused others emphasize that dishonesty and greed, when left unchecked, can result in irreversible damage. His case stands as a cautionary tale about the consequences of unethical actions, reminding us that betrayal and dishonesty, no matter how lucrative in the short term, always carry a price.

"A fool and his money are soon parted."

The learned boast of lineage and name,
But wealth enslaves them just the same.
Gold reigns; virtue is but a claim,
For true greatness is beyond fortune's game.

True Greatness is Beyond Wealth

Do you know the fleeting nature of wealth and the false security it provides? While many people boast of their heritage or wealth, these things do not guarantee true greatness. The poem suggests that wealth and status are temporary, and those who are driven solely by material gain may find themselves enslaved by it. True greatness is not measured by gold or social standing but by inner virtue and character, which are beyond the reach of fortune.

A merchant, rich beyond measure, often boasted of his lineage and wealth. He believed that his wealth defined his greatness. One day, a humble monk approached him and asked, "What is your true greatness?" The merchant replied, "My wealth, my name, my family!" The monk smiled and said, "Gold reigns, but virtue is a claim. True greatness is beyond wealth's game." The merchant, puzzled, decided to follow the monk's teachings. Over time, he learned that his wealth didn't define his worth, and he found true fulfillment in generosity and wisdom. The merchant realized that the essence of greatness lies in what you give, not in what you possess.

Power of Wealth

The Medici family's impact on Florence during the Renaissance is a powerful example of how wealth can shape history. The Medici family, originally bankers, became one of the most influential families in Europe by the 15th century. With vast riches, the Medicis were able to control the politics of Florence, making it a center of culture, art, and political power. Their financial empire funded the work of some of the most famous artists and architects of the time, including Leonardo da Vinci, Michelangelo, and Botticelli. Their patronage of the arts helped birth the Renaissance, influencing the course of Western culture for centuries to come. The

Medici's wealth didn't just support the arts—it also allowed them to exert influence over the political landscape of Italy. They used their resources to manipulate elections, gain power, and even buy influence with the Vatican. Their story highlights the immense power wealth can provide, not just in acquiring material goods, but in shaping culture, politics, and the course of history itself. The Medici family's legacy shows how money, when strategically wielded, can surpass traditional sources of power like military strength or royal lineage, demonstrating how wealth can act as a tool for significant societal influence.

"Wealth is the slave of a wise man. The master of a fool."

A barren cow won't yield, no matter the plea,
Kick it might, but milk there'll never be.
Why ask a miser for generosity?
For true giving springs from the heart, not plea.

True Generosity Comes from the Heart

Seeking generosity from those who are unwilling to give is a futile attempt. Just as a barren cow will never yield milk, a miser will not give freely, no matter how much one pleads. True generosity comes from the heart, not from external pressures or demands. The poem emphasizes that giving with a pure intention is the only form of generosity that has true value. It warns against expecting kindness or charity from those who are not inclined to offer it naturally.

A beggar, desperate for help, approached a wealthy but miserly man, asking for food. The man, though rich, turned him away with harsh words. The beggar moved on, seeking another person, and found a poor woman who, though struggling, gave him what little she had. The beggar thanked her, and she replied, "True generosity is born from the heart, not from wealth." Later, the beggar returned to the rich man, hoping for help, but the man, still selfish, denied him again. The beggar realized that asking a miser for help would never yield results; only those with a generous heart truly give.

Miserly Waste

Hetty Green, often referred to as the "Witch of Wall Street," was one of the wealthiest women in America during the late 19th and early 20th centuries. Despite her vast fortune—estimated at $100 million at the time—Green lived an extraordinarily frugal life. She wore simple, old-fashioned clothing, and refused to spend money on even the most basic luxuries. Her miserly behavior extended to her family, where she reportedly refused to pay for her son's medical treatment when he was injured, leading to permanent harm. Green's life illustrates the futility of hoarding wealth without a purpose or willingness to share it. She accumulated a fortune, but instead of enjoying it or using it for the betterment of others, she lived in near poverty, hoarding her wealth for no apparent reason. Her inability to part with her riches, even when others around her were in need, highlights the emptiness of a life devoted solely to financial gain. Hetty Green's legacy serves as a cautionary tale about the dangers of stinginess, and how hoarding wealth can leave a person spiritually and emotionally bankrupt, despite material success.

"You can't get water from a dry well."

A wealthy man's illness makes world news,
A poor man's wedding gains no views.
The world respects wealth, ignoring virtues,
For true value lies in the soul's hues.

True Value Lies in the Soul

Society always values wealth over virtues and internal worth. The poem highlights how a wealthy man's troubles may be widely recognized, while a poor person's significant life events—such as a wedding—go unnoticed. It points out that true value lies not in external appearances or material wealth but in the inner qualities of a person, such as their soul and virtues. The focus on wealth obscures the deeper, more meaningful aspects of life, which are found in character, integrity, and kindness.

A poor man and a wealthy man were both invited to the same town festival. The wealthy man's arrival was met with grand celebrations and applause. His illness, too, was newsworthy, as everyone in the town talked about it. Meanwhile, the poor man, who had just married the love of his life, found his wedding unnoticed. He went home with a humble heart, knowing the world valued riches more than love. Years later, the wealthy man's fortune faded, and his wealth vanished. The poor man's life, though simple, remained full of joy. The townspeople soon realized that true value was not in wealth but in love, compassion, and kindness.

The Value of Wealth

John D. Rockefeller, often regarded as the wealthiest man of his time, amassed an immense fortune through his oil empire. His wealth allowed him to exert considerable influence on both the economy and society. However, the story of Rockefeller's life also brings into sharp focus the imbalance between his public prominence and the hidden struggles of those who contributed to his empire. While Rockefeller's lavish lifestyle and philanthropic efforts garnered significant attention, the lives of the workers who built his empire remained largely invisible. These laborers toiled under poor conditions for meager wages, their contributions undervalued in the public eye. Rockefeller's wealth allowed him to shape industries and influence the course of American history, but it also highlights the stark contrast between the value placed on wealth and the undervaluation of human labor. The legacy of Rockefeller's fortune prompts us to reflect on how society often celebrates the success of individuals who accumulate wealth, while the often anonymous laborers whose efforts make such wealth possible are overlooked. It is a reminder that true value in society should be recognized in the contributions of all individuals, not just the wealthy elite.

"A man's true wealth is the good he does in the world."

Men of skill and might proclaim,
Even scholars proud of their name,
Bow to gold's unyielding claim,
For wealth controls more than fame.

Wealth Over Wisdom

Wealth has a stronger influence than fame or knowledge. Even those with skill and intellect, including scholars, often bow to the power of gold. It reflects the harsh reality that material wealth often holds more sway than intellectual achievements or renown, as money can shape and control more aspects of life than fame or knowledge.

A renowned scholar, proud of his accomplishments, entered a wealthy merchant's house for a feast. As they dined, the merchant casually offered the scholar a small fortune in exchange for his wisdom. The scholar, though proud of his intellect, knew the power of wealth and hesitated. Finally, he accepted the offer, realizing that even knowledge could be overshadowed by gold. The merchant smiled and said, "Wealth may not buy wisdom, but it buys influence, power, and opportunity. While knowledge is valuable, it is wealth that shapes the world." The scholar learned that while knowledge is precious, wealth holds undeniable power.

Servitude to Wealth

The so-called "Robber Barons" of the late 19th century, such as Cornelius Vanderbilt, John D. Rockefeller, and Andrew Carnegie, wielded immense power in American society, largely through their monopolistic control of industries like railroads, oil, and steel.

These industrialists amassed vast fortunes, but their wealth often came at the expense of workers, who faced grueling conditions and low wages. Despite their achievements in building major industries and contributing to economic growth, these men, despite their apparent success, served the interests of wealth rather than humanity. Their influence was not the result of academic brilliance or social progress, but of an insatiable drive to accumulate wealth. Their focus on personal gain led them to exploit workers, manipulate markets, and use their power to eliminate competition. Even though they were educated and skilled in business practices, they were often blind to the human cost of their actions. The industrial age showed that even the most educated and influential individuals could become servants to wealth, their success measured in dollars and not in moral or social advancement. The Robber Barons' legacies are reminders of how the pursuit of wealth can overshadow other values, transforming what could be a force for good into a tool for exploitation.

"Money makes the world go round."

The listener respects the one who sees,
The wealthy rise above all degrees.
Gold's power towers over these,
But true wealth lies in wisdom's keys.

True Wealth Lies in Wisdom

This poem contrasts material wealth with the true wealth that comes from wisdom. It suggests that while gold and material possessions may grant power and social respect, they do not provide lasting fulfillment or true value. Wealth is fleeting, and those who possess it often fall prey to its corrupting influence. However, wisdom is something that remains, grows, and enriches the soul. True wealth comes from knowledge, understanding, and the ability to make thoughtful, ethical decisions. The poem conveys that while people may praise wealth and its apparent influence, true greatness is found in wisdom, which cannot be measured by wealth or status. Wisdom guides one through life's challenges and provides deeper, more lasting satisfaction than material possessions. The poem calls for a shift in values—away from the pursuit of wealth for wealth's sake and toward the cultivation of wisdom, which brings true richness to life.

A wealthy merchant invited a sage to his home, showing off his grand fortune. "See," said the merchant, "I have everything—gold, land, and power. What more do I need?" The sage, who had little but knowledge and humility, replied, "True wealth does not reside in gold, but in wisdom." The merchant, skeptical, asked, "How can wisdom be more valuable than wealth?" The sage smiled and explained, "Gold can be spent, and power can fade, but wisdom endures and guides you even when wealth and status are gone." The merchant, realizing the truth, understood that wisdom is the most valuable treasure a person can possess.

Value of Experience

The Apollo 11 Mission, which led to the first successful moon landing in 1969, was a remarkable feat of human achievement. However, the success of the mission was not only due to the extensive theoretical knowledge of the astronauts and the engineers at NASA but also to the invaluable experience gained over years of space exploration. The Apollo 11 crew—Neil Armstrong, Buzz Aldrin, and Michael Collins—relied on practical knowledge accumulated from previous missions and simulations, which proved essential when faced with the unexpected challenges of landing on the Moon. While scientific theories and calculations played a key role, it was the ability to adapt and think on their feet, based on prior experiences, that enabled the astronauts to solve unforeseen problems, such as the limited fuel supply and the guidance system malfunctions during the descent. This combination of theory and practice is a powerful reminder that hands-on experience often proves more valuable than purely theoretical knowledge. The Apollo 11 mission is a perfect example of how experience can guide decision-making in high-pressure situations, and how real-world wisdom is crucial to turning ambitious goals into reality. It shows that practical experience, honed through trial and error, often leads to the most successful outcomes.

"Wisdom is the greatest treasure."

Chapter 6

Justice and Morality

Justice ensures fairness, but true justice extends beyond laws to a deeper sense of right and wrong. Morality guides actions, shaping a society where fairness prevails. When justice is upheld, harmony is maintained; when it is compromised, disorder follows. True morality is not about mere rule-following but about understanding the impact of one's actions. Justice demands truth, while morality demands conscience. When both are balanced, societies thrive. However, when personal interests overshadow them, injustice spreads. Upholding justice requires courage, and practicing morality requires wisdom, for these values shape the foundation of a fair and ethical world. The world has witnessed both just rulers like Solomon and tyrants like Nero. Justice ensures order, but morality dictates whether laws serve humanity or oppress it. True justice transcends legal frameworks, aligning with universal ethics and compassion.

If you seize an enemy worthy of strife,
Let mercy, not vengeance, shape their life.
Forgiveness cuts deeper than any knife,
Transforming discord into harmony rife.

Mercy Over Vengeance

True strength lies in forgiveness, not vengeance. Showing mercy to an adversary transforms enmity into harmony, while vengeance perpetuates cycles of conflict. A single act of kindness can heal wounds and pave the way for peace. Forgiveness reflects moral superiority and fosters reconciliation, while revenge, though satisfying temporarily, leaves scars. The poem inspires us to rise above anger and to let compassion guide our actions. Mercy turns foes into allies and proves the transformative power of love over hate.

A knight captured his enemy but spared his life, offering him shelter and food. Moved by this kindness, the enemy swore allegiance to the knight, later saving him in battle. The knight reflected, "Mercy disarms even the fiercest foe." Forgiveness won him a loyal friend and lasting peace.

After World War I, the Treaty of Versailles in 1919 imposed severe penalties on Germany. The nation was humiliated, burdened with heavy reparations, and stripped of its dignity. While the treaty sought to ensure peace, it planted the seeds of resentment. The harsh conditions created a fertile ground for anger and discontent, ultimately leading to World War II.

This chapter in history is a sobering reminder that punishment without understanding can backfire. Had the Allies shown more mercy or balanced their demands with fairness, history might have taken a different path.

The Treaty of Versailles teaches us that true resolution doesn't come from crushing the other side but from fostering understanding and cooperation. When we face conflicts in life, this story reminds us to seek justice tempered with compassion, for the roots of peace lie in the soil of mutual respect.

"To err is human, to forgive divine."

Slaying the poor and looting the land,
Feeding greed with a merciless hand.
Death spares no one, no matter their stand,
For justice is beyond any mortal's command.

Justice Is Beyond Mortal Command

No one can escape justice, no matter how powerful or influential they may be. Exploiting the weak and taking advantage of others for personal gain may seem rewarding in the short term, but the consequences are unavoidable. Greed and cruelty may offer temporary success, but they leave behind a lasting imprint of guilt and regret.

Violence, whether committed out of ambition, selfishness, or sheer disregard for others, ultimately diminishes the one who inflicts it. The pursuit of wealth and power through oppression may create an illusion of control, but it comes at the cost of inner peace. The weight of wrongdoing lingers far beyond the moment of action, suffocating the soul with remorse.

Death is inevitable for all, yet those who have built their lives on harm and deception often find themselves haunted by the consequences of their choices. True justice does not operate on human timelines or according to worldly power—it arrives in its own way and at its own time, beyond anyone's control.

Real strength does not lie in the ability to dominate or exploit but in the wisdom to act with restraint and compassion. The greatest legacy is not one of wealth or influence gained through injustice, but of kindness, fairness, and a conscience free of regret. In the end, only those who choose empathy over cruelty and integrity over greed find true and lasting peace.

The King's Reckoning

In a vast and prosperous kingdom, a ruler sat upon a throne of wealth, built on the suffering of his people. His greed knew no bounds—he seized lands, enslaved the poor, and waged wars to expand his empire. He believed that gold and power made him invincible, that the weight of a crown shielded him from consequence.

One day, a nobleman dared to stand before him and warned, "No throne is eternal, and no ruler escapes justice. The hands of time are impartial, and what you give to the world will one day return to you." The king, amused by the words, dismissed him with laughter.

Years passed, and his wealth only grew, yet his heart remained hollow. One fateful night, as he surveyed his kingdom from his palace, a deep unease settled over him. The echoes of the suffering he had caused seemed to whisper through the halls. He tried to silence them with feasts, but food lost its taste. He sought comfort in gold, but it felt cold in his hands. Sleep abandoned him, and nightmares filled the void.

Then came the reckoning. A rebellion rose from the very lands he had plundered, his soldiers turned against him, and the kingdom crumbled. With nothing left but regret, the once-mighty king wandered in exile, his heart weighed down by the ghosts of his past. In his final days, he realized the truth: true power is not in taking, but in giving, and no wealth can shield a man from the justice of time.

Justice is Inevitable

The Nuremberg Trials, held after World War II, stand as a historic milestone in international justice, reaffirming the principle that no one, no matter how powerful, is above the law. These trials were conducted to hold Nazi leaders accountable for war crimes, crimes against humanity, and the atrocities of the Holocaust, in which six million Jews and countless others were murdered. The trials sent a clear message to the world: individuals—not just governments or military institutions—bear personal responsibility for their actions and can be prosecuted for crimes against humanity.

Among those tried were high-ranking Nazi officials such as Hermann Göring and Rudolf Hess, who played pivotal roles in orchestrating the war and the genocide. Many of the defendants believed that their political influence, military rank, or governmental position would shield them from justice.

However, the trials shattered this illusion, demonstrating that those who commit atrocities cannot evade accountability forever. Some were sentenced to death, while others received long prison terms, reinforcing the idea that justice, though sometimes delayed, is inevitable.

The Nuremberg Trials set a legal precedent that continues to shape international law, laying the foundation for future war crimes tribunals and the establishment of the International Criminal Court. They also established crucial legal principles, such as the idea that "following orders" is not a valid defense for committing crimes against humanity. These trials redefined the boundaries of justice, proving that those responsible for large-scale human rights violations will be pursued, regardless of their status, nationality, or the passage of time.

Beyond their legal significance, the trials served as a moral reckoning, reminding the world that power and cruelty cannot triumph over justice and human dignity. They reinforced the global commitment to ensuring that such atrocities are never repeated. Decades later, the Nuremberg Trials remain a powerful symbol of accountability, standing as a testament to the belief that justice must prevail, even in the face of overwhelming darkness.

"What goes around, comes around."

Chapter 7

Relationships and Bonds

Relationships are built on trust, respect, and understanding. Whether among family, friends, or society, strong bonds create a sense of belonging. However, relationships require effort, patience, and communication to thrive. When nurtured with sincerity, they bring joy and support. When neglected, they lead to distance and misunderstanding. True connections go beyond words—they are strengthened by actions and shared experiences. While some bonds last a lifetime, others fade with time. The quality of relationships matters more than their number, and genuine connections are formed through kindness, empathy, and mutual care. History showcases the power of relationships—whether friendships like that of Krishna and Arjuna or betrayals like Brutus against Caesar. Bonds of love, trust, and loyalty shape personal and political destinies, proving that relationships influence history as much as wars.

If a pot breaks, we can buy anew,
Earthen wares are plenty, tried and true.
But a lost life returns to none's view,
A treasure fleeting, precious and few.

The Irreplaceable Value of Life

Material possessions, like pots, can be replaced, but life is unique and irreplaceable. Each life is a fleeting treasure, precious beyond measure. The poem reflects on the fragility of human existence and the importance of cherishing life. It encourages us to value and protect life, recognizing its profound significance. Unlike objects that can be bought or repaired, life, once lost, leaves a void that cannot be filled. This realization should inspire care, compassion, and an awareness of life's impermanence, urging us to treat each moment and person with respect.

In a village, a potter mourned the loss of his son while his neighbors comforted him by saying, "You can rebuild everything else, but not life." Days later, he saw children playing carelessly near a river and warned them, saving a life. The villagers praised him, and he realized that every life is priceless and worth protecting. From then on, he became a guardian for the children, cherishing the importance of preserving lives.

A Lesson from Ashoka's Transformation

In ancient India, Emperor Ashoka was once known as a ruthless conqueror. His thirst for expansion led to the brutal

Kalinga War, where thousands perished, and the land was soaked in blood.

Victory was his, but the cries of the dying haunted him. He walked among the battlefield's ruins, witnessing not just fallen soldiers but grieving families, orphaned children, and a land stripped of its joy.

One day, as he wandered in deep reflection, he came across an old potter working in a village. The potter shaped clay into fine pots, carefully crafting each one with patience and skill. Just then, a strong wind blew, toppling a row of freshly made pots. Some shattered, while others remained intact. Ashoka watched as the potter sighed but resumed his work, molding new pots to replace the broken ones.

Curious, the emperor asked, "Do you not grieve for your broken pots?"

The potter smiled and replied, "My lord, pots can be remade, but life, once broken, can never be restored. Clay is abundant, but human life is rare and irreplaceable. Unlike pots, we cannot shape a lost soul anew."

Ashoka stood in silence, the weight of his conquests pressing upon him. He had taken countless lives, believing in the power of war, yet here was a simple man reminding him of something greater—life's irreplaceable value. That moment sparked his transformation. He renounced violence, embraced Buddhism, and dedicated his reign to peace, compassion, and the welfare of his people.

The lesson was clear: material things can be replaced, but life is fleeting and precious. From that day forward, Ashoka chose to cherish and protect life, ensuring that his empire would be remembered not for war, but for wisdom and kindness.

Ashoka's Transformation: A Double-Edged Sword of Peace

History reveres King Ashoka as one of India's greatest emperors—not merely for the vastness of his empire, but for the moral depth of his transformation after the bloody war of Kalinga. Witnessing unimaginable destruction and loss of life, Ashoka renounced violence and embraced Buddhism, promoting peace, compassion, and non-violence throughout his realm. His change was monumental, reshaping not only governance but the spiritual fabric of the Indian subcontinent.

But should this transformation be seen as entirely positive? Or did it come with unseen consequences?

Ashoka's decision to abandon war may have brought internal harmony, but it also dismantled the martial spirit of his empire. The Mauryan military, once a formidable force that expanded across Asia, began to shrink in strength and preparedness. Generations of soldiers who had trained for valor were now expected to stand down in the face of aggression, fostering a culture of passivity over protection.

When a kingdom loses its edge to defend its borders, adversaries do not remain idle. After Ashoka's reign, the Mauryan Empire saw a steep decline. In less than 50 years, it crumbled. Historians note a lack of strong successors, but beneath that, perhaps the greater loss was the fading will to fight. The philosophical wave of Ahimsa (non-violence), while noble in spirit, may have unintentionally weakened national resilience.

Peace is powerful. But peace without preparedness is fragile. Ashoka's message of compassion remains timeless, but a nation must also guard its peace with wisdom and strength.

His transformation, though spiritually profound, may have planted the seeds of vulnerability—where silence replaced shields, and tolerance blurred into submission.

In today's world, this historical mirror reminds us: Inner peace is a virtue, but national defense is a responsibility. A sword in the sheath must still be sharp—not for conquest, but for protection.

"Life is priceless."

True kin are revealed when trouble is near,
A soldier's courage shows in the face of fear.
A wife's loyalty surfaces when riches disappear,
For love's depth is tested through sorrow, not cheer.

The True Test of Love and Loyalty

True love and loyalty are tested during challenging times. When life is easy, relationships might seem steady, but it is during hardship, loss, and struggle that the depth of love and loyalty is revealed. The soldier's courage in battle, the wife's devotion during times of poverty, and the support of true kin during adversity all showcase that real bonds are not just about good times but about facing trials together. True loyalty shines when there is nothing left to gain, and all that matters is the bond of love.

A prince, once wealthy and adored, lost his fortune and became a commoner. Many of his friends and advisors turned their backs on him, but his wife stood by him, offering unwavering support. Despite their poverty, she remained by his side, sharing the hardships and maintaining their love.

One day, a wealthy merchant offered the prince riches, but the prince declined, saying, "It's not gold I seek, but the love that has stood the test of time." His wife's loyalty had proved to him that true love is not measured by wealth, but by steadfastness through life's challenges.

Hurricane Katrina devastated New Orleans in 2005, displacing thousands and leaving the city in chaos. In the midst of this calamity, the true nature of relationships was revealed. Some individuals and organizations rushed to provide aid and support, embodying compassion and solidarity. However, others exploited the disaster for personal gain, further deepening the suffering of the victims.

The storm tested friendships, alliances, and communities, showing that adversity uncovers the strength of bonds. Genuine friends and allies went beyond words, offering help without expecting anything in return. Those who took advantage of the situation, on the other hand, were exposed for their selfishness.

This chapter in history teaches us that challenges are a litmus test for relationships. True character is revealed not in times of comfort, but when the world is at its worst. It's in these moments that we discover who we can truly rely on.

"A friend in need is a friend indeed."

Leave unrest, wherever it lies,
An adulterous spouse, or a king unwise.
Abandon what fails to harmonize,
For peace blooms where discord dies.

Releasing What Disturbs Your Peace

Peace is a precious commodity, and anything that disrupts it—whether it's an unfaithful spouse or an unjust ruler—should be let go. Holding onto situations or people that take away your peace leads to internal turmoil. Sometimes, it's necessary to distance ourselves from toxic influences to preserve our well-being. True peace comes when we choose to release what no longer serves us, even if it means leaving behind familiar but harmful situations.

A king was deeply troubled by his queen's unfaithfulness. Her actions caused unrest in the kingdom, and no matter how he tried, he could not find peace. One day, a wise advisor told him, "Peace comes when you release what disturbs it. If your queen is the cause of unrest, you must make the painful decision to part ways, for loyalty and trust are the foundation of peace." The king, though heartbroken, realized the wisdom in the words and chose to let go of the relationship. As he did, the kingdom flourished with harmony, and the king found peace once again.

Leave Toxic Bonds

King Edward VIII's abdication of the British throne in 1936 was a significant and controversial event in history. Edward chose to give up his royal duties to marry Wallis Simpson, an American divorcée, whose relationship with him was considered scandalous by the British establishment. Edward recognized that staying in a toxic, contentious environment would compromise his peace and personal well-being, leading him to choose love and happiness over the burden of the throne.

His decision, although it led to his loss of power, revealed the importance of recognizing when it's time to leave unhealthy situations. Edward VIII's abdication illustrates that sometimes, personal peace and integrity outweigh societal expectations. His life serves as a reminder that relationships and environments that drain us emotionally and spiritually can never lead to true fulfillment. Leaving toxic bonds, whether in love or in career, can be a courageous and necessary step toward self-preservation.

Leaving Toxicity Behind

The Partition of India in 1947, which divided British India into India and Pakistan, was one of the most traumatic events of the 20th century. Millions of people migrated across borders to escape the violence and religious conflict that erupted during the partition. Families who had lived together for generations were forced to leave their homes and their ancestral lands behind. The partition brought with it not only physical displacement but also emotional and psychological scars. The decision to leave toxic environments, marked by communal violence and hatred, was often painful but necessary for survival. The mass migration during this time symbolizes the broader human desire to seek peace and safety, even if it means abandoning everything familiar. People were forced to leave behind their homes, livelihoods, and often their pasts to escape the violence that threatened their lives. The Partition shows how, when faced with destructive forces—be it war, violence, or societal division—people will often choose to leave behind toxicity in search of a better life. The trauma of partition still affects generations, but it also demonstrates the importance of peace and tolerance in a world often divided by difference.

"Let go of what steals your peace; in release, you find tranquility."

The washerman squeezes and cleans each fold,
Ridding impurities, the clothes he'll hold.
What harm, then, if a teacher scolds?
For purification shapes wisdom bold.

The Teacher's Scolding and Purification

This poem draws a parallel between the work of a washerman and the role of a teacher. Just as the washerman cleans clothes by squeezing out impurities, a teacher's scolding or correction serves as a form of purification, removing ignorance and shaping wisdom. The poem emphasizes that criticism, though often difficult, is essential for growth and development. It suggests that, just as the washing process is necessary for clean clothes, correction from a teacher is essential for shaping a student's character and intellect.

A young boy, eager to be perfect, resented his teacher's frequent scolding. He believed it was harsh and unnecessary, and often cried in frustration. One day, his father, noticing his distress, shared a story. "The washerman cleans clothes by squeezing out the dirt. Without this, they remain stained and impure. Similarly, your teacher is helping to cleanse your mind of ignorance." The boy understood that the teacher's corrections were not out of malice, but to guide him towards improvement. Over time, he learned to appreciate the lessons, realizing that criticism, when given with care, is a form of guidance.

The Sculptor and the King: A Lesson in Refinement

In the ancient kingdom of Magadha, a young prince named Jayanta was known for his arrogance. As the sole heir to the throne, he detested criticism and believed himself to be beyond reproach. His father, King Dharma, worried about his future, sought the help of a renowned sculptor, Acharya Varuna.

One day, the king took the prince to Varuna's workshop, where an enormous, unpolished stone lay in the center. "What do you see, my son?" the king asked.

"A worthless rock," Jayanta scoffed.

Varuna smiled and picked up his chisel. "Watch," he said, striking the stone with precise blows. Days passed, and as Jayanta watched, the rough edges chipped away, revealing a magnificent statue of Lord Vishnu.

Amazed, the prince exclaimed, "This is incredible! But why did you strike the stone so harshly?"

Varuna replied, "Without the chisel's sharp edge and relentless strikes, this beauty would remain hidden. Just as a sculptor carves away the roughness of stone, a teacher's correction removes the flaws of ignorance, shaping wisdom and character."

The prince lowered his head in realization. From that day, he embraced his teachers' corrections, understanding that wisdom, like a masterpiece, is shaped through patient refinement.

"A smooth sea never made a skilled sailor."

A raindrop in a shell becomes a pearl,
In water, it blends with the world's swirl.
Destiny decides the fate of each whirl,
For fate's flow shapes every boy and girl.

Destiny Shapes Our Fate

Destiny and fate are the unseen forces that weave the intricate patterns of our lives. Like an artist sculpting a masterpiece from an unshaped stone, these forces mold us, sometimes through gentle whispers and other times through turbulent storms.

Consider a raindrop—one among countless others, seemingly insignificant as it falls from the sky. If it lands in the vast ocean, it dissolves into oblivion. But if fortune guides it into the embrace of an oyster, it undergoes a miraculous transformation, emerging as a radiant pearl. Similarly, life's circumstances, guided by fate, shape us in ways we may never anticipate.

Though we walk our own paths, making choices and forging ahead with determination, we remain part of a grander design—one that often unfolds beyond our comprehension. Like rivers that carve valleys or winds that shape mountains, unseen forces guide our journey, influencing our trials, triumphs, and transformations.

Yet, within this interplay of destiny and free will, there lies an unspoken truth: while fate may dictate where the winds blow, it is our resilience, wisdom, and actions that determine how we sail. Thus, embracing life's uncertainties with courage and grace allows us to turn even the most unexpected turns into opportunities for growth and greatness.

A young boy, born into poverty, dreamed of becoming a great scholar. He studied hard every day, but his circumstances seemed to hold him back. One day, an elder visited the village and told the boy, "A raindrop becomes a pearl when it finds its place." The boy didn't understand at first but later realized that while he could control his actions, his destiny would unfold in its own time. Years later, the boy became a renowned scholar, not because of his circumstances, but because fate had guided him to the right opportunities. He learned that destiny, in its own way, shapes who we become.

Destiny's Role

The assassination of Archduke Franz Ferdinand on June 28, 1914, is widely regarded as the spark that ignited World War I. What began as a seemingly insignificant event—a political assassination—set in motion a series of alliances, treaties, and military mobilizations that ultimately plunged Europe into one of the deadliest conflicts in history. Ferdinand, heir to the Austro-Hungarian throne, was killed by Gavrilo Princip, a member of a nationalist group seeking independence for Serbia. Though the assassination was not part of any grand plan to start a world war, it exposed the fragile and volatile political climate in Europe at the time. A series of diplomatic missteps and alliances soon dragged multiple nations into the conflict, leading to a war that lasted four years and resulted in millions of deaths. The assassination, driven by chance and fate, illustrates how destiny often plays a role in shaping the course of history. Individuals, caught in the winds of fate, can sometimes change the world, but rarely in the way they intend. This tragedy reveals how events beyond control—sometimes as small as a single act—can alter the trajectory of nations, illustrating that some historical shifts are driven not by human action but by destiny itself.

"What is meant for you will not pass you by."

Why marry, why seek heirs?
Family struggles are burdens, who cares?
It's a boulder on life's fragile stairs,
Yet love's true strength makes life fair.

Love and Family Strength

This poem explores the burden and beauty of family life. It begins by questioning the traditional desire for marriage and children, seeing family struggles as burdens that hinder one's progress. The metaphor of family being a boulder on fragile stairs suggests that the responsibilities and challenges of family life can feel heavy and obstructive. However, the poem ultimately reveals that love is the true strength that makes life meaningful and fair. The struggles of family life, while burdensome, are counterbalanced by the love, connection, and support that come with it. Love gives individuals the resilience to endure hardships and the strength to carry life's burdens. It transforms challenges into opportunities for growth and unity. The poem encourages a shift in perspective—rather than viewing family as an obstacle, one should recognize it as the source of strength and love that adds depth and fulfillment to life.

There was a merchant who had made a fortune through his hard work. However, he felt burdened by the responsibilities of marriage and children. He once complained to his friend, "Why should I seek heirs? It's just an additional load in life." His friend replied, "Family is not a burden; it's the source of strength. Love binds us through life's struggles. Without it, life would be empty, and wealth would mean nothing." The merchant took his friend's advice to heart and began cherishing his family. He soon realized that the love and support of his loved ones were the greatest treasures, more valuable than all the riches he had accumulated.

Burden of Family Life

King Henry VIII of England, famous for his six marriages, is a prime example of how poorly managed familial responsibilities can lead to immense personal and political turmoil. Henry's quest for a male heir, along with his complex relationships with his wives, led to a series of political and personal crises. His marriages were motivated by personal desires rather than the greater good of the kingdom, leading to the downfall of several of his wives, political unrest, and eventual break with the Catholic Church. His decision to annul his marriage to Catherine of Aragon and marry Anne Boleyn, among others, sparked the English Reformation and forever altered the course of British history. The emotional and political burdens of his marriages, coupled with the pressure of securing his dynasty, often clouded his judgment and led to a destructive series of decisions. Henry's life shows that the complexities and responsibilities of family life, when poorly managed, can overshadow even the most powerful rulers, and lead to lasting consequences for their kingdoms. It is a stark reminder of the emotional, political, and spiritual burdens that come with trying to balance personal desires with leadership.

"Love makes the world go round."

Count the stars or crush the hills,
Yet, hard hearts defy all wills.
No heat can forge what cold distills,
For only love can melt stubborn ills.

Love as the Power to Transform

In this poem, the power of love is shown as the force that can overcome even the hardest challenges. The comparison of counting stars or crushing hills illustrates how people may attempt to achieve great feats or overcome monumental obstacles, but even these efforts are rendered useless if the heart is hardened. The "hard hearts" refer to individuals who resist change, are impervious to kindness, or who refuse to be moved by love or compassion. No external force—whether heat or effort—can soften a cold heart. Only love has the power to melt stubbornness, prejudice, and hostility. This poem emphasizes that while physical efforts and accomplishments may appear impressive, true transformation happens when love is introduced into the equation. It suggests that love is the ultimate tool for healing and transformation, capable of breaking down barriers and bringing peace where there was once resistance.

There was a young woman who was known for her harsh and unapproachable nature. She often alienated those around her. One day, an elderly woman approached her and said, "You are like a stone in a stream—unyielding and cold." The young woman replied, "I've always been this way, and no one can change me." The elderly woman gently said, "But love has the power to soften even the hardest stone. Open your heart, and you will see how the world transforms." The young woman took the advice to heart and began showing kindness and love. Gradually, she noticed that her relationships improved and the people around her grew warmer and more accepting. She learned that love could break down barriers that her harshness had built.

Nelson Mandela and the Apartheid Regime

For decades, South Africa's apartheid government maintained a brutal system of racial segregation, upheld by laws, weapons, and hard-hearted ideologies. Nelson Mandela was imprisoned for 27 years for resisting it.

Many expected him to emerge from prison full of anger and vengeance. Instead, he came out with forgiveness, humility, and a vision for reconciliation.

Mandela once said, "If I didn't leave my bitterness in prison, I'd still be there."

Rather than using power to crush his enemies, he extended a hand of love and understanding, even inviting his former jailers to his presidential inauguration.

This act of compassion melted even the hardest hearts—leading to a peaceful transition from apartheid to democracy. His truth and reconciliation commission healed countless emotional wounds—not through force, but through love and empathy.

Can love truly change hardened hearts in our current, chaotic world?

It's not easy, but yes, it still works.

Even in today's turbulent world, we've seen leaders and citizens choose empathy over aggression—and change the course of history. We can see Jacinda Ardern's response to the 2019 Christchurch mosque attacks in New Zealand. Instead of reacting with political rhetoric or fear-based responses, she wore a headscarf, hugged victims' families, and addressed the nation not just as a leader—but as a fellow human being. That simple act of compassion reverberated around the world. Hate was met not with hate, but with humane strength. The shooter wanted division. Ardern gave unity.

At a Personal Level, Love Still Wins. We may not all be presidents or revolutionaries, but in everyday relationships—family, friendships, workplace conflicts—love softens more hearts than arguments ever do. A harsh boss may resist pressure, but often a moment of genuine respect or kindness can unlock their better nature.

In some places, power still dominates, cruelty persists, and some hearts remain cold. Love isn't a quick fix. It's a slow, brave fire—not a blazing weapon.

But the world doesn't change through more hatred. It changes when someone dares to love anyway—like Mandela, like Ardern, like countless unnamed peacemakers in families and neighborhoods every day.

It works not always instantly. Not always visibly. But it is the only thing that works deeply.

A candle may not light the whole sky, but in darkness, even one light can guide the lost, warm the cold, and melt the hardest heart.

But one thing remains crystal clear:

If you wish to respond to hatred with love, you must first possess the strength to overcome it by other means if necessary. Love without strength is often mistaken for weakness, and in a world that still respects power, even kindness must be backed by courage.

In India, our deities reflect this balance perfectly. Our goddesses—embodiments of love and motherhood—wield weapons not to destroy, but to protect. Their fierce forms do not contradict their compassion; rather, they uphold it.

Similarly, rulers and authorities must never forget their strength when offering mercy. Compassion must come not from helplessness, but from a place of inner and outer power. Only then will love be respected—not just as a virtue, but as a force capable of transforming even the hardest hearts.

Chapter 8

Pride and Ego

Pride, when balanced, inspires confidence and self-respect. However, when fueled by ego, it blinds judgment and leads to downfall. A healthy sense of pride motivates people to strive for excellence, but excessive pride creates arrogance. Ego resists growth, as it refuses to accept mistakes or listen to others. True wisdom lies in recognizing one's strengths while remaining humble. When pride uplifts, it fosters dignity; when it overpowers, it leads to isolation. Those who control their ego and embrace humility find peace, while those ruled by it struggle with conflicts and dissatisfaction. The rise and fall of figures like Napoleon and Alexander the Great highlight the double-edged nature of pride. While confidence fuels ambition, unchecked ego leads to ruin. Humility, as seen in leaders like Lincoln, fosters lasting greatness.

A cluster fig may look pristine outside,
But within, fig wasps take their pride.
Such is vanity's deceptive tide,
Where truth is masked and shadows confide.

Vanity's Deception

Vanity often presents an alluring facade, much like a cluster fig that appears flawless but hides fig wasps within. The poem warns against being deceived by outward appearances, as they can conceal deeper flaws or emptiness. True value lies in substance, not the superficial. Vanity, though enticing, leads to disillusionment and disappointment. This serves as a reminder to focus on authenticity and integrity rather than being swayed by deceptive exteriors. The truth, though less glamorous, stands strong and unchanging, while vanity's glitter fades, leaving only shadows.

A prince chose a bride based on her beauty, ignoring her character. Meanwhile, his friend, a humble farmer, married a kind-hearted woman. Over time, the prince's wife revealed her selfishness, while the farmer's wife enriched his life with love and support. The prince lamented his choice, realizing too late that true worth lies beyond appearances. Inspired by the farmer's happy life, the prince vowed to value integrity and kindness above vanity.

The Titanic, dubbed the "unsinkable ship," was a marvel of early 20th-century engineering. Its grandeur and advanced design inspired confidence, but this very confidence proved fatal. Believing the ship invulnerable, the designers included only enough lifeboats for half the passengers. On April 15, 1912, the Titanic struck an iceberg, and the "unsinkable" sank, taking over 1,500 lives.

The Titanic's tragedy reveals the dangers of vanity and overconfidence. Superficial pride in technology overshadowed the need for practical safety measures. The story reminds us to stay humble, respect limitations, and always prioritize substance over image.

"Beauty is only skin deep."

Claim the land, and the earth will laugh,
Hoard wealth, and the miser faces wrath.
Flee battle, and death mocks your path,
For nature reclaims what greed cannot grasp.

Nature's Indifference to Human Greed

This poem highlights the futility of human greed and the relentless power of nature. It suggests that no matter how much one claims ownership of land or hoards wealth, nature will ultimately reclaim what cannot be controlled or taken forever. Trying to avoid inevitable struggles, such as in battle, is futile, as fate will catch up with us. It serves as a reminder that human desires cannot alter the natural course of events or the laws of nature.

A wealthy merchant, obsessed with accumulating more land and treasures, thought he could secure his future by hoarding everything he could get. He began taking more than he needed and forcing others off their land. Eventually, nature took its course—floods destroyed his vast estate, and thieves stole his riches. In his last days, he regretted his greed and reflected on his wasted life. The merchant understood that he could not control what nature reclaims: the land and wealth he sought to hoard belong to the earth, greed only leads to loss, and peace comes from living in harmony with nature.

Irony of Pride

Marie Antoinette's extravagant lifestyle, epitomized by her lavish spending and detachment from the struggles of the French people, became a symbol of royal arrogance. Her famous, though likely misquoted, phrase "Let them eat cake" epitomized her indifference to the suffering of the lower classes. Ironically, her pride in wealth and privilege played a key role in her downfall when the French Revolution arose, leading to her execution.

Her tragic end illustrates how pride in one's position can lead to a loss of perspective and eventually to one's demise. Marie Antoinette's refusal to recognize the changing tides of history or the needs of the common people ultimately stripped her of her power. The irony of her situation is clear: her pride in her privileged position was not a shield but a sword that brought her down in the face of growing social unrest. The French Revolution showed that life humbles those who cling to fleeting status, and true strength lies in understanding the needs of others.

"You can't take it with you."

Standing near scholars, can one be wise?
A crane among swans, its disguise belies.
Such pretense, true nature defies,
For wisdom is earned, not a disguise.

Wisdom is Earned

Wisdom is something that cannot be attained through pretension or superficial association. Just as a crane among swans does not become a swan by mere proximity, a person cannot become wise by associating with learned individuals or mimicking their behavior. Wisdom is an internal process that requires personal growth, learning, and reflection. It is earned through experience, self-awareness, and the pursuit of knowledge, not through appearance or external validation. The crane's attempt to mimic the swans highlights the futility of pretending to possess wisdom without truly earning it. Wisdom comes with time, reflection, and life experiences—it cannot be faked or inherited. True wisdom is rooted in understanding one's limitations, learning from mistakes, and continually seeking knowledge. It is a personal journey that requires patience, humility, and the willingness to evolve, making wisdom an earned quality, not a borrowed one.

A young man, eager to be seen as wise, surrounded himself with scholars and intellectuals. He imitated their mannerisms and repeated their words, hoping to be considered learned. One day, an old scholar noticed his pretense and said, "You are like a crane among swans. You may look the part, but wisdom is earned, not assumed." The young man was embarrassed and began to seek true understanding, studying and reflecting on life. Over time, he learned that wisdom comes not from appearances but from genuine knowledge and experience. He realized that true wisdom cannot be borrowed—it must be earned.

Proximity Doesn't Make One Great

King Leopold II of Belgium is remembered for one of the darkest chapters in history—the exploitation and brutal treatment of the Congolese people in the Congo Free State. Despite being surrounded by scholars, philanthropists, and nobles, and presenting himself as a benevolent ruler, Leopold's reign in Congo was a horrific example of greed, cruelty, and exploitation. His ambition to extract rubber and ivory from the region led to widespread atrocities, with millions of Congolese suffering through forced labor, mutilation, and death. Leopold's close proximity to intellectuals and influential figures did not imbue him with the virtues typically associated with greatness, such as compassion, justice, and morality. Instead, he was driven by personal wealth and power, showing that simply being surrounded by greatness or cultured individuals does not automatically confer virtue or moral standing. His actions in Congo serve as a poignant reminder that true greatness comes from the values one upholds, not from the company one keeps. Proximity to greatness, without the corresponding inner goodness, only exposes the depths of one's corruption and lack of humanity.

"Wisdom comes with experience."

Rainless skies bring famine's despair,
Too much rain floods fields laid bare.
Know that both are nature's affair,
For balance in life is a truth we must share.

The Balance of Nature's Affairs

Life is governed by balance—too much of anything can lead to consequences. Just as rain is necessary for life, too much rain can cause devastation. Likewise, too little rain leads to drought and famine. Nature operates on a delicate balance, and understanding this can help us navigate life's challenges. The key to peace and prosperity lies in finding equilibrium, whether it's in nature, relationships, or emotions. Life is not about extremes but about maintaining harmony between opposing forces.

In a village nestled in the mountains, the farmers prayed for rain during the dry season. When the skies finally opened, rain poured heavily, flooding the fields and washing away the crops. The farmers were devastated. An old farmer, wise in the ways of nature, told them, "We prayed for rain, but we must also understand that balance is the law of nature. Too much rain causes floods, too little brings drought. We must accept both seasons and find a way to thrive in each." The farmers learned to respect the balance of nature, realizing that both scarcity and abundance teach valuable lessons about patience and resilience.

Duality of Rain

The Dust Bowl of the 1930s and the subsequent excess rainfall in other regions highlight nature's dual effects—both destructive and life-giving. The Dust Bowl, a period of severe drought, devastated American agriculture, particularly in the Midwest. Massive dust storms ravaged the land, wiping out crops and turning fertile soil into barren desert. Farmers, already struggling with financial hardships, were left with nothing. The drought, caused by a combination of poor farming practices and climatic factors, had a profound impact on the lives of millions. However, in other parts of the country, excessive rainfall led to flooding, causing even more damage. The duality of rain—its ability to nurture or destroy—served as a harsh reminder of nature's unpredictability. While rain is essential for growth, too much can cause destruction, and too little can lead to drought. The Dust Bowl and the floods in other areas show that nature's forces are beyond human control, often acting in ways that are both beneficial and catastrophic. It underscores the need for respect and understanding of the natural world, as well as the importance of sustainable practices to mitigate such extremes.

"Too much of anything is poison; balance is the key to harmony."

The Wisdom of Place

A ship glides gently o'er the ocean wide,
But falters when it meets the rigid shore.
Its strength lies where the swelling currents guide,
Not where the wheels of earth demand it more.

The crocodile in water reigns with pride,
While land-bound dogs might make its power poor.
Each being thrives where nature did decide,
And purpose blooms where roots of strength restore.

Yet man, with pride, forgets his rightful ground,
And seeks to rule where he should walk with grace.
In lands unknown, let reverence abound,
Lest mirrored pride bring ruin in its place.
True wisdom knows when not to make a sound—
It bows to learn, not merely to embrace.

Know your ground, and you will stand firm.

Success is not merely about possessing talent but about applying it in the right environment. A ship glides effortlessly through water, yet it becomes useless on land. Likewise, a crocodile reigns supreme in water but loses its advantage on solid ground. This illustrates a vital truth—abilities, no matter how great, yield the best results only when placed in the right setting.

Recognizing one's strengths and knowing where to apply them is the foundation of true success. Just as the ship belongs to the sea and the crocodile to the river, every individual thrives best when operating within their domain. Misjudging one's capabilities in unfamiliar situations often leads to failure, frustration, and wasted effort. On the other hand, understanding one's element and making the most of it leads to confidence, fulfillment, and achievement.

Life is not just about excelling but about knowing where to excel. Overstepping into unfamiliar territory without preparation can bring setbacks, while respecting one's boundaries and acknowledging others' strengths ensures balance and success. Wisdom lies in recognizing the right place, time, and circumstances to harness one's potential effectively. True fulfillment comes from aligning one's skills with the right opportunities and thriving where one is meant to be.

A talented pianist decided to become a painter but found no success. A friend reminded him, "Your gift lies in music." Returning to the piano, he created symphonies that moved audiences. He realized that success depends on using one's talents in the right place.

In 1927, Charles Lindbergh, a young pilot, made history by flying solo across the Atlantic Ocean. But his achievement wasn't just about flying skills. Lindbergh meticulously prepared, designing a plane that could carry extra fuel, navigating treacherous weather, and timing his journey perfectly. His success was a combination of skill, preparation, and the right opportunity.

Lindbergh's story teaches us that talent alone isn't enough. You can be the best at what you do, but without the right context and preparation, success can remain elusive. It's about knowing when to act and being ready when the moment arrives.

His historic flight reminds us to hone our skills and wait for the right opportunity. Success, like Lindbergh's flight, is a journey of persistence, preparation, and courage.

Hannibal Barca, the brilliant Carthaginian general, was a master of strategy. During his legendary campaign against Rome, he shocked the ancient world by crossing the Alps with an army that included war elephants. These majestic beasts were symbols of strength, capable of terrifying enemies on the battlefield. However, as the terrain grew harsher, the same elephants became a burden. They struggled to navigate the cold, narrow mountain paths, and many perished before reaching the battlefield.

Hannibal's campaign demonstrates an important truth: even the strongest assets can falter if placed in the wrong context. Strength is not absolute—it must align with the environment to be effective. Hannibal's story reminds us to assess situations carefully and adapt our strengths to the context. Just as the elephants needed a battlefield, our talents thrive in the right conditions. The key is to know where and how to apply them.

In India, do as the Indians do.

Pride in familiar surroundings can lead to downfall in unfamiliar territories. Just as even a giant ship seems small in the reflection of a mirror, wisdom lies in adapting to one's environment. Arrogance in unknown situations often leads to embarrassment, while humility earns respect and understanding. Whether in a foreign land or new circumstances, bending with grace rather than resisting with pride ensures survival and success. The poem underscores the virtue of humility, reminding us that flexibility and openness create bridges where pride builds walls.

A boastful tiger crossed into a neighboring forest, declaring itself king. However, it was unfamiliar with the terrain and fell into a hunter's trap. A kind elephant helped free the tiger, advising, "In new lands, humility wins favor, not pride." The tiger learned to approach unfamiliar situations with respect and care.

In 1893, a young lawyer named Mohandas Gandhi was traveling in South Africa when he was thrown off a train for refusing to give up his first-class seat, despite holding a valid ticket. That moment of humiliation could have broken his spirit. Instead, it became a turning point. Gandhi chose not to respond with anger or pride but with humility. He reflected on the injustice he faced and began to develop the philosophy of nonviolent resistance that would later change the world.

This experience teaches us that adversity doesn't define us—our response to it does. Gandhi's humility wasn't weakness; it was a quiet strength that transformed his pain into a powerful movement. His story reminds us that even in the face of discrimination, choosing humility and reflection can lead to profound change. It's not always about fighting back but about standing firm in your principles and letting your actions speak louder than your words.

When Doors Open Blindly

When gates swing wide to strangers, hearts untried,
And lands embrace with unexamined grace,
The roots may rot beneath the nation's pride,
While smiling masks may wear a shifting face.

A garden blooms when tended from inside,
But weeds invade when keepers lose their place.
No fortress stands if watchful eyes have died—
Soft welcomes may invite a harsh disgrace.

What once was peace may tremble into dust,
When foreign feet reshape the native ground.
A bond of trust must first be earned by trust,
Not forced by words or promises unbound.
A land is lost not always with a thrust—
But when its soul forgets its sacred sound.

It is always right not to allow immigrants to settle in one's own land. If they are not at all loyal they act loyally and they show their originality when they get an opportunity. it is already showcased in many countries now a day. To avoid the misconceptions, here I am going to illustrate an imaginary story.

A Tale of Migration and Consequence

In the early 1990s, the war-torn country of Zudora saw thousands of its citizens fleeing to the neighboring nation of Eldoria. Among them was Rafiq, a young man with dreams of building a new life. He settled in the capital city, working tirelessly in construction and sending money back home. Over time, more Zudorans followed, forming a close-knit community in the heart of Eldoria.

At first, their presence was welcomed. The migrants took jobs that locals often ignored—cleaning streets, working in factories, and laboring on farms. Eldoria, in desperate need of workers, saw an economic boost. But as the years passed, tensions began to rise. The migrants, still loyal to their homeland, created self-sufficient enclaves, refusing to integrate into Eldorian society. They maintained their language, traditions, and even their own governance within certain districts.

As their numbers grew, so did the challenges. The schools in migrant-dominated areas struggled to accommodate children who didn't speak the local language. Crime rates increased as some unemployed youth turned to illicit activities. Eldorians, feeling marginalized in their own country, began protesting. The government, caught between humanitarian concerns and national interests, introduced stricter immigration policies, sparking further unrest.

Then came the boiling point. A radical faction within the Zudoran migrant community, still bitter over their homeland's past conflicts, started spreading anti-Eldorian sentiments. A series of violent clashes erupted, leading to riots in the city. Businesses were torched, streets became battlegrounds, and the once-welcoming Eldorians now saw migrants as a threat.

The government responded with mass deportations, but it was too late to undo decades of division. The cycle of migration, opportunity, resistance, and conflict had already reshaped

Eldoria forever. What had begun as a humanitarian crisis had morphed into a political and social struggle—one that neither side had foreseen, but both had to endure.

Migration is a double-edged sword. When integration fails, divisions emerge. A balance between compassion and national stability is essential to ensure that migration strengthens rather than fractures a society.

The Fall of the Aztec Empire to Hernán Cortés (1519–1521)

When the Spanish conquistador Hernán Cortés arrived in the Aztec Empire (modern-day Mexico), the native emperor Montezuma II welcomed him, believing Cortés might be a god or a divine figure.

Instead of forming a genuine alliance, Cortés exploited the trust, gathered intelligence, used internal dissent among native tribes, and ultimately toppled the Aztec civilization. This event led to colonization, massive loss of life, culture, and the forced imposition of foreign rule and religion.

Chapter 9

Spirituality and Divinity

Spirituality is a journey inward, seeking meaning beyond material existence. It is not confined to rituals but involves self-awareness, inner peace, and connection with the universe. Divinity is experienced in moments of stillness, kindness, and purpose. While beliefs may differ, the essence remains the same—finding truth within and living with harmony. A spiritually aware person looks beyond external success and seeks fulfillment in wisdom and compassion. Whether through meditation, prayer, or reflection, spirituality enriches life by guiding one toward self-realization and balance. It is a path that transcends boundaries and leads to deeper understanding. Spirituality has guided civilizations, from the teachings of Christ to the meditations of the Buddha. True divinity is found in selflessness and wisdom.

A spoon of sacred milk suffices well.
What's a pot of donkey's milk to tell?
A full plate of virtue satisfies the spell,
For purity nourishes the soul's swell.

The Value of Purity

One should understand the importance of purity in life. A small amount of sacred milk, representing virtue and goodness, is far superior to a large quantity of something impure, like donkey's milk. True satisfaction comes from quality, not quantity, and purity nourishes the soul in a way that excess, devoid of integrity, cannot. We should focus on cultivating genuine virtues and meaningful actions, rather than pursuing superficial abundance. By valuing the essence of what is good and pure, we enrich our inner lives and achieve true fulfillment.

A chef prepared a meal with fresh, quality ingredients, while his apprentice used a large quantity of inferior ones. When served, the chef's small dish delighted guests, while the apprentice's large platter remained untouched. The chef explained, "It's not the size but the purity and effort behind the work that counts." Inspired, the apprentice began focusing on quality in his cooking and life, understanding that even a small act, done with sincerity and purity, holds greater value than abundance without substance.

Michelangelo's work on the Sistine Chapel ceiling stands as a testament to human perseverance, artistic genius, and unwavering dedication. Commissioned by Pope Julius II, this monumental task was not only physically exhausting but also mentally and emotionally taxing. Painting for four long years, often lying on his back under the vast ceiling, Michelangelo transformed an ordinary space into a celestial vision, bringing biblical stories to life with breathtaking detail and grandeur.

Despite the immense pressure to complete the project swiftly, Michelangelo refused to compromise on quality. Every stroke of his brush bore the weight of his commitment to excellence. He toiled through discomfort, sculpting figures in paint with the same precision he would have carved them in marble. His work was not just about fulfilling a commission but about creating something that would inspire generations—an enduring testament to human potential.

Michelangelo's story is more than an artistic triumph; it is a profound lesson on the pursuit of mastery. In an age obsessed with speed and instant results, his dedication reminds us that true excellence is never rushed. Quality demands patience, resilience, and an unyielding devotion to one's craft. Just as the Sistine Chapel ceiling remains an immortal masterpiece centuries later, the impact of well-crafted work—whether in art, science, or any field—transcends time.

Greatness is not measured by how quickly something is completed, but by the depth of effort and passion invested in it. Michelangelo's legacy teaches us that when we pour our heart and soul into our endeavors, we do not merely create—we leave behind something eternal.

"Quality over quantity."

God does not dwell in distant lands,
He resides within, close at hand.
Seek Him quickly; obey His command,
For He is near, in heart and sand.

The Presence of God Within

God is not far away, residing in distant realms, but is close at hand, residing within the hearts of all. There is no need to search far and wide; the divine is always near, within us and all around us, in the sand beneath our feet and in the very core of our being. The poem encourages an immediate and personal connection with God, urging individuals to seek Him within and follow His guidance, for He is always present and ready to be found.

A pilgrim traveled far to find a temple where he believed God would be most powerful. After years of searching, he returned weary and disillusioned. His teacher asked him why he searches so far for what has always been within you and guided him in meditation, helping him discover a deep sense of peace and connection with the divine within. The pilgrim realized that he had been looking outward when God had always resided within. From that day on, he sought the divine in every moment, finding peace in every breath.

Mother Teresa, often referred to as the "Saint of the Gutters," dedicated her life to serving the poorest of the poor in Calcutta. To her, every person in need embodied the divine. She believed God was present in each human soul, especially in those suffering.

Her acts of kindness were small but transformative. Whether holding the hand of a dying leper or providing shelter to an orphan, her service was marked by humility and an unwavering belief in the value of every life. When praised for her work, she would simply say, "I am a pencil in God's hand."

Mother Teresa's life reminds us that divinity is not found in grand gestures or places of worship but in acts of love, compassion, and service. By recognizing the humanity in others, we discover the presence of God within ourselves.

"God dwells within."

What can be done will find its way,
What cannot will never obey.
Divinity's will differs from our sway,
For fate's design flows in its own way.

The Unstoppable Flow of Fate

Fate and divinity have a path that cannot be altered by human will. What is destined will occur, and what cannot happen will never come to pass. It suggests that human efforts, no matter how strong, cannot change the greater design of fate. The poem emphasizes the inevitability of life's course, which flows according to its own divine plan, and that trying to control it is futile.

A king, proud of his abilities, tried to defy the prophecy that his reign would be short-lived. He built great walls, raised powerful armies, and made preparations to resist fate. Despite his best efforts, a natural disaster struck the kingdom, leading to the downfall of his rule. The king, realizing that his efforts to fight destiny had failed, consulted a wise man. The man said, "What is meant to happen will happen, no matter how hard you fight it. Fate's design cannot be altered by human will." The king finally accepted the inevitability of fate and ruled the remainder of his days with wisdom and humility, no longer attempting to control the uncontrollable.

Divine Will

The Apollo 13 mission in 1970 stands as one of the most remarkable feats in human history. The mission's original goal was to be the third manned lunar landing, but the astronauts faced a life-threatening crisis when an oxygen tank exploded, crippling the spacecraft. The explosion caused a loss of vital resources, leaving the crew with no viable options. Mission control in Houston scrambled to come up with solutions, knowing the odds of survival were slim. Despite the meticulous planning and expertise of both the astronauts and the engineers, there was only so much they could do. The crew's survival depended on their quick thinking, faith in one another, and a stroke of divine intervention. In the end, the astronauts returned safely to Earth, defying expectations and highlighting the limitations of human control in the face of unforeseen forces. The story of Apollo 13 teaches us that, no matter how prepared we are, we are often at the mercy of forces beyond our understanding, be they divine or simply unanticipated events. The mission, often seen as a "successful failure," is a testament to human resilience, ingenuity, and the belief that, at times, fate has a hand in the outcomes we can't control.

"Man proposes, God disposes."

Say one thing, but harbor another,
When actions and thoughts fail to tether,
Can one expect grace to gather?
For truth aligns the heart like no other.

Truth Aligns the Heart

This poem emphasizes the importance of authenticity and alignment between one's words, actions, and thoughts. The core message is that when someone's actions do not align with their spoken words, they cannot expect to earn grace, respect, or goodwill from others. True grace and sincerity can only be achieved when the heart, mind, and behavior are in harmony. If one says one thing and acts differently, they create discord within themselves and with others, making it difficult for grace to flow naturally. It suggests that truth is the foundation for inner peace and external harmony. When we live truthfully, aligning our actions with our beliefs, we build a strong character that draws respect and divine grace. Thus, the poem calls for honesty, transparency, and consistency in both thought and deed, for these qualities bring inner fulfillment and are deeply rooted in personal integrity.

A merchant known for his charming words was admired by many. However, his actions often contradicted his speech, as he frequently deceived customers to make a profit. One day, a wise traveler visited his shop and listened to his sales pitch. The traveler, knowing the merchant's true nature, said, "You speak of honesty, but your actions tell a different story." The merchant, ashamed, asked how he could change. The traveler replied, "Align your words with your actions. Only then will grace and respect follow you." The merchant realized that truth is the only path to genuine success, both in business and life.

Hypocrisy and Divine Grace

The French Revolution of the late 18th century was a time of great upheaval, as the people of France rose against the monarchy in pursuit of liberty, equality, and fraternity. However, many of the revolutionaries who championed these ideals were themselves guilty of hypocrisy. Leaders like Maximilien Robespierre, who preached about justice and equality, became embroiled in the Reign of Terror, overseeing executions of thousands, including political opponents. The hypocrisy of these leaders became apparent as they, too, were intoxicated by power, abandoning the very principles they had once fought for. This contrast between their ideals and their actions ultimately led to their fall from grace. The revolution, which began with the promise of liberty, became tainted by the same vices it sought to eliminate. The French Revolution, while instrumental in shaping modern political thought, also highlighted how easily power and hypocrisy can corrupt noble ideals. In the end, the revolutionaries' loss of public trust demonstrated how the disconnect between preached ideals and actions can lead to a loss of credibility and divine grace. Their actions serve as a warning about the dangers of hypocrisy, especially when leaders fail to live by the principles they espouse.

"Actions speak louder than words."

A frog survives, sealed in stone,
Who feeds it, when it's alone?
The Creator never leaves His own,
In solitude, His grace is shown.

Grace in Solitude

This poem highlights the concept that even in the most isolating moments, grace is still present. The frog trapped in stone symbolizes individuals who may seem isolated, abandoned, or forsaken, yet the divine presence is always near. No matter the circumstances, the Creator does not abandon those who seek solace in solitude. In solitude, one may feel disconnected from others, but this is a time when divine grace is often revealed more clearly. The poem suggests that God's presence is not dependent on external conditions or the company of others; rather, it is deeply rooted in the individual's heart. The message is that grace can be experienced in moments of quiet reflection, when we are at peace within ourselves. Solitude becomes an opportunity to connect with the divine and grow spiritually. In such moments, we realize that our connection with God is never truly severed, no matter our external situation.

A young monk, feeling forsaken in his hermitage, questioned why he had been left alone. One evening, as he prayed in solitude, a vision of light appeared to him. The vision spoke, "Even in isolation, I am with you. It is in silence and solitude that you can hear my voice the clearest." The monk realized that his loneliness was not a punishment but an opportunity to connect deeply with the divine. He embraced his solitude, knowing that grace is not always found in the company of others but in moments of quiet reflection and spiritual connection.

God as the Provider

The Lascaux Cave Paintings, discovered in southwestern France, are among the most significant archaeological finds of the 20th century. These ancient artworks, created by early humans around 17,000 years ago, depict scenes of hunting, animals, and symbols of nature. The paintings not only offer insight into early human culture but also highlight the spiritual beliefs of these ancient peoples. It is believed that these early humans saw the divine hand in nature and regarded God or a higher power as the provider of sustenance and protection. The cave paintings show scenes of hunting and animal symbolism, suggesting that these early humans saw nature and the divine as inseparable, with the success of their hunts being linked to divine favor. In a world without modern science or technology, early humans relied heavily on nature for their survival and placed their trust in divine forces to ensure their well-being. These ancient artworks serve as a testament to the deep spiritual connection early humans had with nature, believing that God or a higher force played a direct role in providing for their needs. The Lascaux cave paintings remind us of the universal human belief in divine provision, which transcends time and culture.

"Stillness is the key to peace."

Man builds idols with pride and art,
Yet ignores the God within his heart.
Seek Him within, and play your part,
For the divine resides where love starts.

Seek God Within

The people often look outside of themselves for spiritual fulfillment, but true spirituality begins from within. The act of building idols or seeking God in external symbols may be a way to find connection, but the essence of divinity resides within the human heart. The metaphor of man building idols represents the superficial search for spirituality, often through outward symbols or practices, while ignoring the deeper, inner spiritual connection. True divine presence and peace are found by looking within, embracing love, and cultivating an inner relationship with the Creator. The poem urges readers to recognize that the divine does not reside in objects or external rituals but in the love, compassion, and sincerity they foster within themselves. The essence of God is within each individual, and the path to spiritual enlightenment is through inner reflection, self-awareness, and the cultivation of love and kindness toward all.

A king sought guidance from a renowned priest, asking how he could please God. The priest gave the king a golden idol, saying, "Worship this, and you will find grace." However, the king did not feel fulfilled and continued to search for peace. One day, he met an old man who told him, "The Creator does not live in idols or gold. Seek the divine in your heart, in love and kindness toward others." The king, realizing the truth, turned inward, offering kindness and love to all. He soon found the peace he had sought—within himself.

Misplaced Worship

The Protestant Reformation, sparked by Martin Luther's 95 Theses in 1517, brought about profound changes in the Christian Church and in the way individuals viewed their relationship with God. One of the central issues that Luther and other reformers addressed was the Catholic Church's focus on rituals, indulgences, and the worship of saints, rather than fostering a direct and personal connection with God. Luther criticized the church for placing too much emphasis on outward rituals and material wealth, which he believed distracted from true faith. His challenge to the church's practices led to the creation of new Protestant denominations that emphasized personal scripture reading, prayer, and a direct relationship with God. The Protestant Reformation thus marked a shift from external forms of worship to internal spirituality, encouraging individuals to look inward and question the validity of practices that seemed to obscure the true essence of faith. Luther's efforts were not just about rejecting the Catholic Church, but about a reformation of how people approached their spiritual lives, rediscovering the concept of inner divinity and personal connection with God. His criticisms ultimately led to a re-evaluation of Christian spirituality, which emphasized individual faith over the rituals of the Church.

"The kingdom of God is within you."

With cheese in hand, unsure of ghee,
Man prays to idols, blind to divinity.
The self is where God ought to be,
For true worship lies in authenticity.

True Worship Lies Within

This poem speaks to the illusion of external rituals in religious worship and emphasizes the importance of internal devotion. The metaphor of holding cheese but unsure of ghee reflects how people may offer outward symbols of worship, such as rituals or idols, without understanding or truly connecting with the divine. The poem critiques the practice of praying to idols while being blind to the divine presence within oneself. It stresses that true worship is not about external gestures but about recognizing the divine within. The self, not idols or external symbols, is where God truly resides. Worship, in its truest form, is about authenticity, self-awareness, and aligning one's life with divine principles. The poem calls for a deeper, more personal connection to spirituality, suggesting that the essence of devotion lies in understanding and embracing the inner divinity that exists within every individual.

Once, a great king decided to visit a temple to offer his prayers. He wore his finest robes, brought lavish gifts, and performed every ritual perfectly. Afterward, he asked a wise sage about the true meaning of worship. The sage replied, "True worship isn't in the rituals you perform or the gifts you bring; it lies in how you treat others and honor the divine within yourself." The king realized that he had been focusing on external acts and neglected the inner peace and purity that truly define worship.

He spent the rest of his life striving to live in harmony with his inner self and others.

Forgetting Inner Divinity

Ramakrishna Paramahamsa, a 19th-century Indian mystic, taught that the divine is not something to be sought externally but is inherently present within every individual. His teachings focused on the importance of recognizing the inner divinity that resides in all people, urging his followers to look within themselves for spiritual enlightenment rather than seeking it in external rituals or distant gods. Despite his deep spiritual insights, Ramakrishna observed how many people, especially in the materialistic age, neglected this inner spiritual essence. Instead, they sought divinity in external symbols, idols, or distant sources, forgetting that the divine spark lies within. Ramakrishna's message challenged the prevailing religious practices of his time, urging people to discard superficiality and seek truth within their own hearts. His teachings remind us that true spirituality arises from self-awareness and the realization of the sacred within, rather than from external sources of power. In a world where many continue to search for meaning in external objects or externalized beliefs, Ramakrishna's wisdom urges us to turn inward to discover the profound divinity that resides within each of us.

"What you do is more important than what you say."

Chapter 10

Silence and Words

Words have the power to heal or hurt, to inspire or destroy. Silence, on the other hand, speaks in ways words cannot. Knowing when to speak and when to remain silent is a mark of wisdom. While words express thoughts, silence allows for reflection. Meaningful words can uplift, while careless ones create conflicts. Silence can be powerful when used with purpose, offering space for clarity and understanding. True communication is not just about speaking but about listening. In the balance between silence and words lies the key to meaningful interactions and deeper relationships. History proves that silence can be powerful, as seen in Gandhi's nonviolent resistance, while words have the force to ignite revolutions, like Martin Luther King Jr.'s speeches.

The Ganges flows serene and deep,
While drains roar where filth may seep.
The noble endure; the weak cannot keep,
For stillness holds what chaos cannot reap.

The rivers flow, deep and steady,
A stream, erratic, rushes heady.
Should the wise stoop to the fool's ready?
True wisdom flows calm, never petty.

Wisdom in Calmness

A deep, steady river flows with quiet strength, carrying life and sustenance without demanding attention. Its calm surface hides immense power, reflecting resilience, wisdom, and purpose. In contrast, a noisy, rushing stream or drain, though loud and restless, carries little of true substance. It is fleeting, stirred by every small disturbance, and ultimately dissipates without leaving a lasting impact.

This contrast mirrors the nature of true wisdom and superficial noise. A wise person, like the deep river, remains composed and unwavering, choosing to act with intention rather than react to every passing distraction. They understand that strength is not found in loud declarations but in quiet perseverance. Just as the river nurtures life without seeking recognition, a person of depth influences the world through steady, meaningful actions rather than empty clamor.

On the other hand, those who lack wisdom are often quick to react, engaging in meaningless disputes and wasting energy on trivial matters. Their presence is marked by disorder, much like a stream that rushes wildly but ultimately loses its course.

True intelligence is not measured by the ability to argue or make noise but by the capacity to remain still in the face of chaos, choosing clarity over confusion and patience over impulse.

In a world filled with distractions, it is easy to be drawn toward the clamor of shallow disturbances. However, those who cultivate inner stillness, much like the deep river, find the strength to endure and make a lasting impact. Silence, when rooted in wisdom, is not a sign of weakness but of profound understanding. The strongest forces in nature—and in life—do not need to shout to be heard.

In a bustling city, a quiet woman named Meera meditated by the riverside every morning. The nearby market was full of quarrels and shouts, yet Meera remained serene. One day, a curious child asked, "Why don’t you join the noise?" Meera replied, "The river teaches me to flow steadily, even when storms rage above." Years later, during a town crisis, it was Meera's calm wisdom that helped the community find solutions, while others panicked. Her composed nature earned her respect, proving that peace endures where chaos fails.

Once, a sage sat by a river, watching its steady flow. A young man approached, eager to debate, challenging the sage with many questions. The sage remained silent, letting the water flow without interruption. The young man, impatient and energetic, kept pressing for an answer, but the sage simply pointed to the river. He said, “Like the river, wisdom flows quietly and steadily. A rushing stream may seem loud, but it lacks depth. True wisdom doesn't seek attention, it remains calm and steady, unaffected by the foolishness of others." The young man understood that wisdom is not loud or impatient but quiet and composed, like the steady flow of a river.

Mother Teresa dedicated her life to serving the poor in the slums of Calcutta. Without grand speeches or public fanfare, she quietly fed the hungry, cared for the sick, and comforted the dying. Her actions were small but consistent, creating a profound impact. Much like the silent flow of the Ganges, her kindness quietly nurtured the lives of those she touched.

In a world often obsessed with noise and spectacle, Mother Teresa's life reminds us of the power of silence. It's not the loud proclamations that change lives but the quiet, selfless acts of love. Her story inspires us to focus on deeds rather than declarations, proving that even in the absence of noise, we can create echoes that last forever.

Difference Between Greatness and Foolishness

Martin Luther King Jr. was known for his eloquent speeches that called for peace, justice, and equality in a time of racial tension in the United States. His speeches, filled with dignity and hope, contrasted sharply with the hateful rhetoric of those who opposed civil rights, including figures who used violent and divisive language. King's greatness lay in his ability to remain calm, steady, and focused on the greater good, even in the face of enormous challenges. His speeches were not just calls for social change but reflections of his deep moral conviction and belief in non-violence. In contrast, his adversaries, who often resorted to hate speech and violence, exemplified foolishness. Their words, fueled by fear and ignorance, only deepened divisions and stoked animosity. King, through his measured and thoughtful speeches, demonstrated that true greatness is not found in rash words or impulsive actions, but in the ability to stand firm in one's principles, without resorting to hatred or violence. His leadership exemplified the power of calm, rational thought and compassion in the face of hatred and prejudice. The contrast between King's peaceful rhetoric and the chaos of hate speech underscores the difference between true greatness and the folly of divisiveness.

"Still waters run deep."

The word of many finds acceptance wide,
A single voice may be denied.
Neutral words hold no side,
For truth's power cannot be compromised.

The Power of Truth Over Popularity

The poem speaks to the difference between widespread acceptance and the enduring power of truth. While many voices may be accepted and celebrated, a single voice may be silenced if it speaks uncomfortable truths. Neutral or false statements often find acceptance because they avoid controversy. However, the poem emphasizes that truth is not subject to popularity; it is powerful in its own right, standing firm even if it is unpopular or denied. It reminds us that the value of truth is not defined by its acceptance but by its unwavering authenticity.

A wise philosopher in a small town spoke truths that were uncomfortable for many to hear. At first, he was dismissed, and his ideas were ignored. However, over time, his words began to resonate with the people. Eventually, they realized that his teachings, though hard to accept, were grounded in truth and led to lasting change. The philosopher's unwavering commitment to truth, despite initial rejection, left an indelible mark on the town. The people learned that, while popular opinions may change, truth remains steadfast and powerful, even in the face of resistance.

Collective Words Matter

The Suffragette Movement in the early 20th century was a powerful example of how collective voices can spark profound societal change. Women across the world, united in their demand for voting rights, fought against oppressive systems. Their unified efforts, despite facing resistance and oppression, ultimately led to the passing of laws granting women the right to vote.

This movement demonstrated the strength of collective action and the transformative power of words when they are spoken with unity. The suffragists' rallying cries for equality and justice reached the hearts of many and proved that when people come together with a common purpose, their voices can change the course of history. Their struggle is a reminder that our words, especially when spoken in solidarity, can have a lasting impact on society.

"Truth will out."

With words of silk, let your voice enthrall,
A gentle tongue can conquer all.
Like golden waves, let kindness flow,
And watch how fortunes start to grow.

The Art of Persuasion

The way we speak holds immense power over how others perceive and respond to us. Words, when spoken with charm and warmth, can create strong connections, win trust, and even open doors to opportunities. People are naturally drawn to those who express themselves with grace and positivity, as pleasant speech fosters goodwill and influence.

Moreover, skillful communication isn't just about conveying information; it's also about persuasion. Those who master the art of speaking can navigate social and professional situations more effectively, earning admiration and even material rewards. This idea suggests that success is not merely about knowledge or hard work but also about how one presents their thoughts and emotions to the world.

In a bustling town, there lived a wealthy but shrewd merchant named Dhanraj. He was known for his sharp business skills but had a harsh tongue that often drove customers away. One day, as he sat outside his shop, an old beggar approached him and said, "Sir, may I share a secret that can double your fortune?"

Intrigued, Dhanraj smirked and said, "What can a beggar teach a rich man?"

The beggar smiled and replied, "Watch and learn." He walked to a nearby fruit vendor, spoke a few kind words, and received a handful of fresh fruits for free. Then, he approached a jeweler, complimented his craftsmanship, and was gifted a small silver ring.

Dhanraj was astonished. "How did you do that?" he asked.

The beggar chuckled, "Words are like gold when spoken sweetly. People love to give to those who respect and appreciate them. Your wealth comes from trade, but true fortune comes from how you speak."

Dhanraj took the lesson to heart. From that day, he greeted customers with warmth and spoke with charm. Soon, his business flourished like never before, not just because of his goods but because people enjoyed dealing with him.

Chanakya and the Power of Speech

In ancient India, during the reign of the great Mauryan Empire, lived a brilliant scholar and strategist—Chanakya. He was not only an expert in politics and warfare but also in the subtle art of influence through words. His wisdom shaped the destiny of Chandragupta Maurya, turning him from a mere peasant boy into a mighty emperor.

One day, a young scholar approached Chanakya with great eagerness. "Guru, I have studied scriptures, philosophy, and warfare, but I still struggle to gain influence. What is the true secret to success?"

Chanakya, instead of answering directly, called for two bowls—one filled with honey and the other with neem juice.

He handed the honey bowl to the young man and said, "Taste this."

The scholar dipped his finger and tasted it. "Sweet and pleasant," he said with a smile.

Then, Chanakya offered the bowl of neem juice. The scholar hesitated but took a sip. Instantly, his face twisted in disgust. "Bitter and unbearable," he coughed.

Chanakya chuckled and asked, "If I were to offer you more honey, would you accept it?"

The scholar nodded eagerly.

"And what if I gave you more neem juice?" Chanakya asked.

The scholar shook his head. "Never again, Guru! It is too bitter to swallow."

Chanakya placed both bowls aside and looked at him with piercing eyes. "My child, words are like these two bowls. A man who speaks with grace, wisdom, and kindness attracts people just as honey attracts bees. But one who speaks harshly, with bitterness and arrogance, repels others just as neem repels the tongue."

He continued, "A king does not conquer his subjects by force alone. He first wins their hearts with words. A merchant does not sell goods by mere display but by persuasion. A wise man does not command respect through power but through the sweetness of his speech."

The scholar pondered over this lesson and asked, "But what if one must speak the truth, even if it is bitter?"

Chanakya smiled. "Even bitter medicine is given with honey, my son. If truth must be spoken, let it be wrapped in kindness and wisdom, so it is accepted rather than rejected."

The young scholar bowed in gratitude. From that day forward, he practiced speaking with charm and persuasion, carefully choosing his words. Years later, he became a respected minister in the royal court, using his wisdom and eloquence to resolve conflicts, influence decisions, and win the trust of kings and commoners alike.

"A sweet tongue weaves fortune, while a harsh one shatters trust."

Pot, vessel; hill, mountain's frame,
Salt is sodium, by another name.
Though tongues differ, the truth's the same,
For reality holds no room for blame.

The Truth That Transcends All Names and Differences

While words and names may differ from language to language, the essence of truth remains constant. Just as a pot is still a pot and salt remains salt, no matter what we call them, truth is the same everywhere. In life, people may speak different languages or follow different customs, but the underlying reality—the truth—remains unchanging. Reality does not bend to our labels or beliefs, and truth is not subjective. It stands firm, no matter how we try to define or categorize it.

In a busy town, there were many debates about which religion, philosophy, or practice was superior. People argued endlessly, each claiming their path was the truest. One day, an old man gathered the people and said, "What is truth? A pot is a pot, whether you call it a 'vessel' or 'container.' The truth is the same for all, even if the names differ. It is not in the labels we give things, but in their essence." They were quiet, realizing that all their arguments were based on names, while the truth transcended these differences. The old man taught them that reality holds no room for division, and that truth is universal.

Different Words, Same Essence

Universal scientific principles like gravity demonstrate how the essence of truth remains the same across different languages and cultures. While the term "gravity" may differ in various languages, from "gravité" in French to "gravedad" in Spanish, the fundamental force it describes is universal. This unity of truth across languages highlights the consistency of the natural world and the interconnectedness of human understanding. Despite linguistic barriers, the concept of gravity is understood by people around the globe, and its effects can be observed universally. This phenomenon serves as a reminder that while languages may vary, the core principles of nature remain constant and accessible to all. Whether someone speaks English, Hindi, Mandarin, or any other language, the force that causes an apple to fall to the ground applies equally. The global unity of scientific truths like gravity underscores the shared nature of human knowledge. No matter the words used, the essence of these principles transcends language, showcasing the unity of truth in the scientific world.

"Truth is one; the names are many."

Chapter 11

Hardships and Adversity

Adversity is an inevitable part of life, testing strength, patience, and perseverance. While hardships may seem overwhelming, they often bring growth and resilience. Challenges shape character, teaching lessons that comfort never can. Those who endure difficulties with courage emerge stronger and wiser. Hardships reveal inner potential, pushing people beyond limitations. While suffering can be painful, it also fosters understanding and empathy. Overcoming struggles requires determination and faith in one's abilities. In the end, adversity is not meant to break but to build, transforming obstacles into stepping stones toward success and self-discovery. Adversity has shaped history's greatest minds—Abraham Lincoln's struggles, Helen Keller's perseverance, and Mandela's resilience. Hardships test endurance and character, proving that true strength is forged in the fires of difficulty.

An iron rod, broken, a smith may repair.
A shattered heart defies the craft's care.
Lost love is beyond any mender's fare,
Its echoes linger in silent despair.

Irreparable Loss

Some losses, particularly of love and trust, leave wounds that no external effort can mend. A smith may repair a broken rod, but a shattered heart resists even the most skilled hands. The echoes of lost love linger, reminding us of its fragility and the pain of neglect or betrayal. This poem underscores the importance of cherishing relationships and handling emotions with care. Once trust or love is broken, it is challenging, if not impossible, to fully restore. The silent despair of a broken heart teaches the value of genuine connection and the pain of its absence.

A sculptor worked tirelessly to create a statue, but a careless helper dropped it, shattering it. Though the sculptor repaired it, cracks remained visible. Later, the sculptor quarreled with his closest friend, ending their lifelong bond. Reflecting on the statue, he realized that while physical objects could be mended, relationships required deeper effort and sincerity. He sought forgiveness, but his friend, too hurt, refused. The sculptor lived with the regret, learning too late that love, once broken, leaves lasting scars.

The Partition of India in 1947 was one of history's most heartbreaking events. Millions were forced to leave their homes, crossing newly drawn borders amidst chaos and violence. Families were torn apart, friendships shattered, and lives uprooted. The physical wounds healed over time, but the emotional scars lingered, leaving generations to grapple with the pain of separation.

Unlike broken objects, the wounds of broken hearts are not easily mended. The Partition's legacy reminds us of the human cost of division and the enduring power of empathy and unity. It challenges us to work toward understanding and reconciliation in a world that often seeks to divide. In remembering the pain of the past, we are reminded to cherish the bonds that hold us together and strive for a future where no heart must break for the sake of borders.

"Trust, once broken, is hard to rebuild."

Pebbles in shoes, flies in ears,
Thorns in feet bring silent tears.
Discord at home breeds endless fears,
For internal strife dims the light of years.

Internal Discord Dims the Light of Life

Inner strife and unresolved issues are like small but persistent irritations that disrupt peace and joy. Pebbles in shoes, flies in ears, and thorns in feet symbolize the discomfort caused by internal discord. Such conflicts—whether within oneself or in relationships—bring silent suffering, affecting the overall well-being of an individual. Peace of mind is essential for happiness, and unresolved internal struggles can overshadow the light of life, leading to perpetual discomfort and fear.

A man, always grumbling about his external circumstances, wondered why he felt unhappy despite having everything he desired. One day, he went to a wise elder for advice. The elder, noticing the man's unrest, invited him on a walk. As they walked, the elder casually pointed out the pebbles in the man's shoes and the flies buzzing around his ears. The man immediately stopped and tried to fix these minor inconveniences. The elder smiled and said, "You see, these small irritations make your journey unpleasant. So too, does inner conflict, no matter how small, disrupt your peace." The man realized that resolving his inner turmoil was the key to finding true happiness.

Small Aggravations

Marie Curie's dedication to science led to groundbreaking discoveries in radioactivity, but her path was far from smooth. In the early stages of her career, Curie faced numerous challenges, many of which seemed small in isolation but compounded into immense personal struggles. As a woman in a male-dominated scientific field, she had to contend with discrimination and a lack of recognition. Funding for her research was scarce, and she often had to rely on small, makeshift laboratories and rudimentary equipment. Despite these obstacles, Curie's resolve never wavered. Her work, which eventually earned her two Nobel Prizes, changed the course of science. However, the toll these small aggravations took on her physical health was significant, as prolonged exposure to radiation ultimately led to her death from leukemia. Curie's story highlights the persistence needed to overcome minor yet accumulating obstacles. Her journey reminds us that achieving greatness often requires overcoming countless small irritations and setbacks, and that perseverance in the face of adversity is essential for scientific and personal breakthroughs.

"A house divided against itself cannot stand."

Hunger bows to no man's law,
Darkness sees sincerity withdraw.
In anguish, pride suffers its flaw,
For humility is strength, not a mere law.

Humility in Suffering

The strength comes from humility in times of hardship. While hunger and suffering do not respect a person's wealth or status, true strength is found in humility, not pride. When faced with difficulty, pride fades, and humility allows a person to endure with grace. The poem implies that the true nature of strength lies in how one navigates suffering, choosing humility over arrogance, regardless of external circumstances.

A rich merchant, accustomed to luxury, fell ill and was bedridden for months. During his illness, he encountered many people—some with compassion, others with scorn. The wealthy merchant, once proud and arrogant, learned the hard way that his riches could not shield him from suffering. He noticed how humble villagers, struggling with their own burdens, endured hardship with grace and humility. He realized that true strength wasn't in his wealth or position but in how one responds to suffering. When he recovered, he began to live more humbly, offering help to others without pride. His wealth didn't matter anymore; humility had become his true strength.

Hunger and Anguish

The Bengal Famine of 1943 remains one of the most harrowing examples of how hunger can strip away the dignity of individuals and communities. During this time, millions of people in Bengal, India, faced extreme food shortages due to a combination of poor governance, war-induced disruptions, and natural calamities. As the situation grew dire, once-proud and dignified people were driven to acts of desperation. Hunger consumed their rationality, leading them to steal, fight, and even resort to cannibalism in the most extreme cases. The famine revealed the fragility of human society when survival instincts take over. Societal norms and the boundaries between right and wrong broke down as people sought any means to feed themselves. The anguish of the famine was not just physical but psychological, as the people of Bengal were left to grapple with the loss of their humanity in the face of unrelenting hunger. The famine serves as a poignant reminder of how the most basic human needs—like food—can cause profound societal disruption and personal suffering when they are not met. It also underscores the importance of governance and social responsibility in preventing such tragedies.

"Humility is the solid foundation of all virtues."

Even mothers may shun their kin,
When fortune fades and poverty sets in.
Truth reveals who stands within,
For love's true test is when trials begin.

True Love in Adversity

True love and loyalty are not about comfort or wealth; they are tested through adversity. When fortune fades and poverty sets in, many people may abandon their loved ones, seeking greener pastures. However, the true test of love and loyalty is when one's circumstances change, and only those who stand by you in times of struggle are the ones who truly care. Love is not based on what one can offer materially, but on the strength of character and compassion shown when times are hard.

Once, a wealthy merchant named Ravi had a flourishing business and many friends. However, a series of misfortunes led to his downfall, and soon, he was left with nothing. His friends, who had once depended on his wealth, began to ignore him. His mother, too, turned distant, for she had always enjoyed the comforts that his wealth provided. But one person, his childhood friend Arvind, never wavered. Arvind helped Ravi without hesitation, sharing the little he had. Ravi, at first, felt humiliated by his loss, but Arvind's unwavering support became a source of strength. Eventually, Ravi managed to rebuild his life, not through wealth, but through the genuine love and loyalty of those who stood by him in his time of need.

Harsh Reality of Poverty

Vincent van Gogh, one of the most influential artists in history, spent much of his life in poverty, struggling both financially and emotionally. His genius was largely unrecognized during his lifetime, and he lived in near destitution, often relying on his brother, Theo, for financial support. Despite his immense talent, van Gogh's art failed to bring him the fame or fortune he sought, and his poverty led to social isolation. The harsh reality of his financial struggles exacerbated his mental health issues, contributing to his eventual breakdown and tragic death. Van Gogh's life highlights how poverty can isolate individuals, stripping them of both social support and personal stability. His story is a poignant reminder that financial hardship is not just an economic issue but a social one as well, deeply affecting mental and emotional well-being. The struggles of van Gogh show that talent and genius do not always guarantee success or recognition, and that poverty can keep even the most brilliant minds from achieving their full potential. His legacy, while ultimately celebrated, serves as a somber reminder of the ways in which poverty can diminish an individual's quality of life, even when they possess extraordinary talents.

"True friendship is tested in times of trouble."

Welcome a mean soul into your space,
And suffering follows, a bitter embrace.
A fly's entry can upset the place,
For negativity spreads in its trace.

The Spread of Negativity and the Power of Positivity

Negativity has a powerful impact—it can spread quickly and disrupt the peace of an entire environment. Just as a fly's presence can upset the tranquility of a room, inviting negative individuals into your life can cause suffering and unrest. On the other hand, positive energy and kind-hearted people bring peace and joy. It's important to be selective about who we allow into our lives, for their energy will influence our own.

In a peaceful village, the arrival of a mean-spirited man caused unrest. He spread rumors, sowed discord, and created tension between the villagers. The once-harmonious community was soon filled with suspicion and anger. The village elder, seeing the damage, gathered the people and said, "Like a fly that disturbs a room, negativity can ruin the peace we have. We must not allow such energy to enter our lives. Instead, let kindness and patience flourish." The villagers learned to avoid those who brought negativity and focused on fostering peace among themselves.

Welcoming Trouble

The Trojan Horse, a pivotal element in Greek mythology, symbolizes the danger of welcoming something seemingly harmless that ultimately brings devastation. According to the myth, during the Trojan War, the Greeks built a giant wooden horse and left it as a "gift" outside the gates of Troy. The Trojans, believing it to be a symbol of peace, brought the horse inside their city. Unbeknownst to them, Greek soldiers were hidden inside. During the night, the soldiers emerged from the horse, opened the city gates, and allowed the Greek army to invade. The Trojan Horse illustrates how an outwardly innocent or even benevolent gesture can hide a dangerous intention. It serves as a cautionary tale about the risks of accepting things at face value without understanding their true nature. In many aspects of life, from personal relationships to politics, inviting something or someone into one's life without caution can lead to unintended consequences. The Trojan Horse is a metaphor for how, sometimes, the things we think will bring peace and prosperity can, in fact, lead to conflict and destruction if we do not question their true purpose.

"Negativity spreads like wildfire; protect your peace from its flames."

Chapter 12

Folly and Ignorance

Ignorance is not merely the absence of knowledge but the refusal to seek truth. Folly arises when one clings to assumptions without questioning or learning. Many mistakes in life stem from acting without understanding or making judgments without clarity. The wise embrace learning, while the ignorant resist it. True growth comes from admitting limitations and striving for awareness. Folly leads to repeated failures, but wisdom guides toward better choices. Recognizing ignorance is the first step toward enlightenment. The more one learns, the more one realizes how much remains to be understood. Mistakes repeat when ignorance prevails. The fall of the Roman Empire and economic depressions remind us that folly, when unchecked, leads to destruction. Learning from history prevents the cycle of ignorance from continuing.

The Folly of Hoarding

The tale of King Midas is a timeless cautionary story. Granted a wish by the god Dionysus, Midas chose that everything he touched turn to gold. At first, he delighted in his newfound power, turning objects into shimmering treasures.

However, his joy soon turned to despair. Food and water became inedible gold, and when his daughter embraced him, she too transformed into a lifeless statue. Midas realized his greed had robbed him of life's true treasures: love, sustenance, and joy. Desperate, he begged Dionysus to reverse the curse, learning too late that hoarded wealth without purpose leads to ruin.

This story reminds us that happiness doesn't lie in accumulation but in appreciating life's simple, essential gifts. It warns against the emptiness of greed and teaches the value of balance and gratitude.

Put a dog's tail in a pipe; it'll stay till it's freed.
The vice-ridden never alter their creed.
Attitudes remain, no matter the deed,
For a heart of stone will never take heed.

Ingrained Vices

A person's shortcomings, negative mindset, or undesirable habits cannot be altered by external influences alone; true transformation begins from within. No amount of persuasion, pressure, or external circumstances can bring about a meaningful change unless the individual consciously acknowledges the need for improvement and commits to it. Bad habits and stubborn behaviors tend to persist because they become ingrained over time, making it difficult to break free from them without deliberate effort.

Even when faced with challenges, consequences, or advice from others, a person's internal outlook remains unchanged unless they genuinely desire to shift their perspective. The power of change lies in self-awareness, determination, and consistent effort. Only when an individual takes responsibility for his growth and actively works toward improvement can achieve lasting transformation. True change is not imposed from the outside—it emerges from a deep, personal willingness to evolve and strive for betterment.

A young man, known for his bad temper, was given advice by a wise elder: "If you do not free your heart from anger, it will be like a dog stuck in a pipe—stubborn and unyielding." The young man ignored the advice, thinking time would change him.

However, years passed, and he found himself alienated and alone, with no peace. He returned to the elder, asking for guidance. The elder simply said, "The pipe is your heart, and you are the dog. Only you can free yourself." From then on, the young man worked on controlling his temper, understanding that true change must come from within.

Al Capone, the notorious gangster of the 1920s, spent much of his life building a criminal empire through bootlegging, racketeering, and violence. Despite multiple arrests and imprisonments, Capone never abandoned his criminal ways. Even when incarcerated, he continued to run his operations, highlighting how deeply ingrained vices can be.

Capone's life illustrates the difficulty of breaking free from destructive behaviors and habits. His relentless commitment to crime, even in the face of severe consequences, shows that deeply rooted tendencies can be hard to change.

This story serves as a reminder of the importance of recognizing and addressing negative patterns before they become entrenched. While change is always possible, it requires conscious effort and the willingness to confront the vices that hold us back.

"You can lead a horse to water, but you can't make it drink."

Critics find fault with others' flaws,
Yet they stumble over their own cause.
Blind to their faults, they misplace applause,
For true vision comes when ego withdraws.

Fault-Finders

This poem exposes the hypocrisy of critics who are quick to find fault in others but fail to acknowledge their own shortcomings. The critics are blind to their own flaws, and in their arrogance, they fail to see the truth. It suggests that true vision and understanding come not from judging others but from humbling oneself and recognizing one's own imperfections. The poem encourages self-reflection, urging individuals to withdraw their ego and focus on their own faults before criticizing others.

A well-known critic who constantly pointed out the flaws of artists was invited to an exhibition of his own work. The paintings he displayed were poorly done, and when he was asked about them, he became defensive. One artist, who had been the subject of his harsh criticisms, gently said, "A critic sees flaws in others, but the greatest art is in accepting one's own flaws." The critic, embarrassed, began reflecting on his own actions and words. He realized that true understanding comes not from pointing fingers but from humility and self-awareness. From that day, he became more compassionate and thoughtful in his critiques.

In the 1950s, Senator Joseph McCarthy led a campaign to accuse hundreds of Americans of being communists, often based on flimsy evidence or no evidence at all. His accusations led to public fear and ruined the lives of many innocent people. McCarthy was quick to find faults in others, but when his own flaws were exposed, he could not acknowledge them.

McCarthyism serves as a cautionary tale about the dangers of self-righteousness and the failure to reflect on one's own shortcomings. It shows how a focus on finding fault in others can blind us to our own flaws, leading to a toxic culture of accusation and paranoia.

This period in history teaches us that judgment should be tempered with self-reflection. Instead of criticizing others, we must examine our own actions, ensuring that we hold ourselves to the same standards we set for others. Without self-awareness, we risk perpetuating injustice in the name of righteousness.

"People who live in glass houses should not throw stones."

Don't jest with kings, their wives, or fire,
Don't play with weapons or their ire.
Such pranks lead to outcomes dire,
For arrogance stirs the wrath of the pyre.

The Consequences of Arrogance and Ignorance

This poem warns against arrogance and disrespect towards powerful or dangerous entities, such as kings, their families, or fire. It emphasizes that such recklessness can lead to dire consequences. The metaphor of "pranks" and "ire" suggests that foolish actions against authority or danger, whether it's a monarch or a volatile situation, can ignite anger and lead to destruction. It serves as a reminder that humility and caution are key when dealing with powerful forces, whether human or natural.

A young man, eager to prove his bravery, mocked the king's wife during a royal event. His jests were heard by the queen, who, deeply insulted, informed the king. Enraged by the disrespect, the king sentenced the man to exile. The young man realized too late that his arrogance had sparked the wrath of power. In a distant land, he came to understand that, like fire, some forces cannot be played with without consequences. He returned, seeking forgiveness, having learned that humility and respect are crucial when dealing with authority and power.

The tale of the Trojan Horse is a cautionary story about the dangers of deceptive actions. The Greeks, unable to breach the walls of Troy after a long siege, built a massive wooden horse and hid soldiers inside. They left it as a supposed gift to the Trojans, who, believing it to be a symbol of surrender, brought it into their city. That night, the Greek soldiers emerged and opened the gates to allow their army to invade, leading to the fall of Troy.

The Trojan Horse serves as a warning about the dangers of hidden motives and deceptive gestures. What appeared to be a harmless act—a gift—concealed a deadly intent. This story teaches us that pranks and deceitful actions, even when masked as fun or harmless, can lead to catastrophic consequences. It highlights the importance of being cautious and discerning, especially when something seems too good to be true.

"Don't poke the tiger."

A dressed-up monkey rules its kin,
A crown on a fool still lies thin.
The worthless gather where none win,
For vanity thrives where truth has been.

Vanity and the Fool's Crown

The poem critiques vanity and how it elevates those who are undeserving. A dressed-up monkey or a fool crowned with royalty highlights that appearances can be deceiving. The poem suggests that true worth is not in outward trappings, but in inner qualities like wisdom, humility, and integrity. The fool, adorned with a crown, still lacks the wisdom to lead, and those who follow him are bound to fail. It serves as a reminder that vanity and superficial appearances often mask the absence of true value.

A king once appointed his son as his successor, due to his handsome looks and charisma, despite his lack of wisdom. The people rejoiced, believing the crown signified greatness. But soon, the prince's decisions caused harm to the kingdom. A wise old man advised the king, "A monkey in royal robes is still a monkey." The king, realizing the folly of choosing vanity over wisdom, replaced his son with a capable advisor. The prince, though outwardly regal, had no true skill to lead. The people learned that true leadership lies in wisdom, not in appearances.

Unworthy Gatherings

Emperor Nero's reign was marked by indulgence, excess, and a lavish court filled with sycophants who flattered him instead of challenging his actions. Nero's inner circle, composed of unworthy companions, amplified his worst tendencies and surrounded him with praise rather than accountability. This environment contributed to Nero's tyranny, as his power was unchallenged, and his decisions became increasingly erratic.

The consequences were disastrous for both the emperor and the Roman Empire. Nero's self-absorbed leadership, encouraged by the sycophantic members of his court, ultimately led to his downfall. His inability to see through the flattery of his companions resulted in poor decision-making, which hastened his decline. Nero's court serves as a lesson in the dangers of surrounding oneself with individuals who only mirror one's own desires and fail to provide honest, constructive feedback. Without genuine counsel, leaders can spiral into destructive patterns, as seen in Nero's reign.

"Appearances can be deceptive."

Sandalwood smeared on a donkey's skin,
It kicks in ignorance, unaware within.
The unworthy cannot grasp value's spin,
For true essence lies beyond the skin.

The Ignorant and Their True Essence

Outward appearances may create an illusion of refinement, but they can never truly change a person's inherent nature. Just as smearing a donkey with sandalwood paste may give it an air of elegance, its fundamental ignorance and nature remain unchanged. In the same way, a person devoid of wisdom, integrity, or virtue cannot be defined by external embellishments such as fine clothing, wealth, or status. True character is not shaped by outward appearances but by one's inner qualities, values, and moral compass.

Superficial transformations may deceive the eye, but they do not bring about real growth or enlightenment. True worth is not found in material possessions or temporary facades but in a person's depth of understanding, kindness, and ethical conduct. A shallow display of refinement may impress momentarily, but it is the substance within—the wisdom, integrity, and sincerity of a person—that determines their true value. Ultimately, real transformation occurs from within, and no amount of external decoration can substitute for genuine character and virtue.

A wealthy merchant bought a donkey and covered it in fine silks, hoping to impress his neighbors. He paraded it through the streets, expecting admiration for its beauty. But the people, recognizing the donkey for what it was, simply laughed. The merchant was frustrated and asked a wise man for advice. He replied, "No matter how much you adorn a donkey, it will always remain a donkey unless it learns wisdom." The merchant realized that true worth cannot be masked with decoration and that only internal growth could bring true respect.

Misunderstood Value

Galileo Galilei faced intense opposition when he proposed the heliocentric model of the solar system, which suggested that the Earth revolved around the Sun. His discovery, supported by his telescope observations, was met with ridicule and condemnation, particularly from the Catholic Church, which upheld the geocentric model. His revolutionary ideas were undervalued and rejected by those unwilling to accept new truths.

Galileo's experience highlights the difficulty that visionary ideas often face in the face of established authority and tradition. The Church, like a donkey failing to appreciate the sandalwood, failed to recognize the value in Galileo's work, stubbornly clinging to outdated beliefs. His legacy, however, proves that true knowledge and understanding can withstand the resistance of those who fail to adapt. Galileo's perseverance in the face of scorn eventually led to a paradigm shift in our understanding of the universe, underscoring the importance of embracing new perspectives.

"You can't polish a turd."

Greed is misery, unmatched and stark,
Without wisdom, joy finds no spark.
Without focus, success leaves its mark,
For the heart devoid of truth is cold and dark.

Greed and Lack of Wisdom Lead to Misery

The poem highlights the destructive nature of greed, illustrating that it brings misery and darkness into one's life. Greed, when paired with a lack of wisdom, destroys the potential for joy or success. The poem emphasizes that wisdom is the key to happiness and fulfillment. A heart devoid of truth and integrity remains cold and distant, incapable of experiencing genuine joy or success. The message warns that materialism and selfish desires do not lead to true satisfaction.

A young man, fixated on accumulating wealth, neglected his relationships and personal growth in his pursuit of riches. He bought lavish possessions and lived in luxury, but he felt empty inside. One day, an old friend visited him and asked, "Do you feel truly happy?" The young man, surrounded by his wealth, realized that, despite all his possessions, he felt no joy. His greed had led him to forsake everything that truly mattered. In that moment, he decided to shift his focus from accumulating wealth to seeking wisdom and true fulfillment. He learned that wisdom and a generous heart bring true happiness, not greed.

Greed and Ignorance

The 2008 financial crisis was a direct result of unchecked greed and ignorance in the financial sector. Banks, investors, and lenders engaged in high-risk behavior, promoting subprime mortgages to individuals who were unlikely to repay them. The rapid rise in home prices led to a bubble, with many buying homes they couldn't afford, while banks bundled these bad loans into securities and sold them to unsuspecting investors. When the bubble burst, the financial system collapsed, causing a global economic meltdown. The crisis exposed how greed—combined with a lack of understanding of the risks involved—could lead to widespread disaster. The financial institutions that caused the crisis were more concerned with short-term profit than long-term stability, and as a result, millions of people lost their homes, jobs, and savings. The 2008 crisis serves as a powerful reminder of the dangers of unchecked greed, and how ignorance of the consequences can have devastating effects on individuals and entire economies. It also highlighted the need for greater transparency and accountability in financial institutions to prevent such crises from happening again.

"Greed is a bottomless pit that only leaves you wanting more."

Unaware of life's truth, people craft creeds,
Bringing pain to others through selfish deeds.
A dog barks at its reflection; its ignorance leads,
For understanding lies beyond blind needs.

Ignorance Leads to Suffering

Ignorance often leads individuals to act against their own best interests without realizing the truth of their actions. When people fail to see reality as it is, they create unnecessary conflicts, divisions, and misunderstandings, harming both themselves and others. Much like a person reacting to an illusion, they remain trapped in their own misconceptions, believing falsehoods to be truths. This blindness stems from selfishness, fear, or an unwillingness to question deeply ingrained beliefs.

True understanding can only be attained when one steps beyond these limitations and perceives the world with clarity. Wisdom is not merely the accumulation of knowledge but the ability to see beyond surface appearances, recognizing what is real and what is illusion. It requires self-awareness, open-mindedness, and the courage to let go of preconceived notions. Only when a person overcomes their narrow perspective and embraces deeper insight can they act with true wisdom, fostering harmony instead of division and understanding instead of ignorance.

A village was divided by conflicting beliefs. People built walls of judgment, rejecting others' views without truly understanding them.

One day, a wise man came to the village and witnessed the discord. He observed how each group fought over their own version of truth, ignoring the broader reality. He asked the villagers to gather and showed them a dog barking at its own reflection in the water. "The dog cannot see that it is only itself it barks at," he explained. "In the same way, your ignorance and pride keep you blind to the truth. True understanding comes when you look beyond your own reflection." The villagers, realizing their error, sought peace.

Creation of Divisions

The Crusades, a series of religious wars between Christians and Muslims, are one of the most tragic examples of how ignorance and power struggles can create deep divisions between cultures and societies. Beginning in the 11th century, the Crusades were ostensibly launched to reclaim Jerusalem from Muslim rule, but they quickly expanded into broader conflicts, with religious and political motivations intertwining. Christians and Muslims, who had coexisted in various regions for centuries, were suddenly pitted against each other in a violent and bloody struggle. The Crusades led to centuries of warfare, mistrust, and cultural divide between the two religious groups. The wars not only caused the loss of countless lives but also intensified the hatred and suspicion between Eastern and Western societies. The Crusades serve as a potent reminder of how divisions based on religious misunderstandings and political power can lead to long-lasting suffering and conflict. They highlight the dangers of allowing ignorance, fear, and unchecked power to dictate the actions of societies, as such divisions often leave deep scars that endure for generations.

"Ignorance is the mother of all conflict."

Chapter 13

Anger and Desires

Anger and desires are natural emotions, yet when uncontrolled, they lead to suffering. Anger clouds judgment, making people act impulsively, while unchecked desires create restlessness. When guided wisely, desires can inspire ambition, but when excessive, they turn into greed. Suppressing anger is not the solution; mastering it is. Similarly, desires should be balanced with contentment. True peace is found in self-control, where emotions are acknowledged but not allowed to dominate. Those who master their anger and desires find clarity, while those ruled by them struggle with regret and dissatisfaction. History records the devastating effects of unchecked desires, from the Trojan War to colonial conquests driven by greed. Anger fuels revolutions but also destruction. Controlling impulses leads to progress, as seen in the discipline of great leaders.

A fish is hooked by the bait's lure,
Its desires lead to downfall sure.
So man's greed destroys his core,
Leaving his soul hollow, lost evermore.

Greed's Downfall

Greed, like a baited hook, lures individuals into their own downfall. Just as a fish's desire blinds it to danger, human greed can lead to destruction, leaving one spiritually hollow. The poem warns against succumbing to desires that trap and harm us, emphasizing the need for contentment and self-restraint. Greed never satisfies; instead, it consumes and corrodes, taking more than it gives. True fulfillment comes from understanding and cherishing what we already have. The poem calls for wisdom and balance, steering us away from the perils of unchecked desires.

A wealthy man was obsessed with expanding his riches, ignoring his health and family. One day, he saw a monkey caught in a trap, its hand stuck while clutching a piece of fruit. Unable to let go, the monkey remained trapped. Realizing the parallel with his own greed, the man freed the monkey and reflected on his life. He began to let go of unnecessary desires, focusing on his family and well-being, finally finding peace and joy in simplicity.

The Rise and Fall of Enron: A Cautionary Tale of Corporate Greed

Enron Corporation was founded in 1985 through the merger of Houston Natural Gas and InterNorth, a natural gas company.

Under the leadership of CEO Kenneth Lay, Enron transformed itself from a traditional energy company into a global powerhouse in energy trading, telecommunications, and even broadband services. By the late 1990s, Enron was seen as one of the most innovative and successful companies in America.

The company pioneered the use of energy trading, allowing companies to buy and sell electricity and natural gas as commodities. This innovation, coupled with aggressive expansion, made Enron a darling of Wall Street. The company's stock soared, and at its peak in August 2000, it was trading at $90 per share, with a market capitalization of over $60 billion.

The Illusion of Success

Behind the scenes, however, Enron's success was built on a web of deceit. The company, along with its chief financial officer Andrew Fastow, used complex accounting loopholes, special purpose entities (SPEs), and fraudulent financial reporting to hide its debts and inflate profits.

One of the key tactics involved "mark-to-market accounting," where Enron would record projected future profits from long-term contracts as if they were actual earnings. If a contract turned out to be less profitable than expected, the losses were hidden in off-the-books partnerships controlled by company insiders. This created an illusion of continuous financial growth while, in reality, Enron was accumulating massive undisclosed debt.

Meanwhile, Enron executives, including Kenneth Lay and CEO Jeffrey Skilling, encouraged employees and investors to buy Enron stock, even as they secretly sold their own shares, knowing the company was in trouble.

The Unraveling of the Scandal

In 2001, analysts and journalists began questioning Enron's financial statements, particularly its lack of transparency. The first major red flag came when Enron's Chief Financial Officer, Andrew Fastow, was found to have conflicts of interest in the partnerships that were hiding Enron's debts.

As pressure mounted, Enron was forced to admit that it had overstated its earnings by nearly $600 million. The company's stock plummeted, and by December 2001, Enron declared bankruptcy—the largest corporate bankruptcy in U.S. history at the time.

Investors lost billions of dollars, and thousands of Enron employees who had invested their retirement savings in company stock were left with nothing. Meanwhile, top executives walked away with millions, having cashed out their stock before the collapse.

Legal Consequences

The scandal led to multiple criminal investigations.

Jeffrey Skilling, the former CEO, was convicted of fraud and insider trading and sentenced to 24 years in prison (later reduced to 14 years).

Kenneth Lay, the company's founder, was convicted of conspiracy and fraud but died of a heart attack before sentencing.

Andrew Fastow, the CFO, pleaded guilty to fraud charges and was sentenced to six years in prison.

The Enron scandal also led to the dissolution of Arthur Andersen, one of the largest accounting firms in the world, which was found guilty of obstructing justice by shredding Enron-related documents.

The Aftermath and Lessons Learned

The Enron collapse was a wake-up call for corporate America and resulted in sweeping regulatory reforms. In 2002, the U.S. Congress passed the Sarbanes-Oxley Act (SOX), which established stricter rules for corporate financial reporting, increased penalties for fraud, and required greater accountability from executives.

The Enron scandal remains one of the most infamous examples of corporate greed and ethical failure. It serves as a stark reminder that unchecked ambition, when coupled with deception, can lead to catastrophic consequences—not only for those who perpetrate fraud but also for innocent employees, investors, and the broader economy.

True success, as Enron's downfall illustrates, is not measured by short-term financial gains but by long-term integrity and trust.

"Greed leads to grief."

Anger robs greatness, leaving regret,
Unbridled rage brings pain unmet.
Control your temper; your goals will be set,
For patience is the key to peace, not fret.

Anger and Patience

The destructive nature of uncontrolled anger is to hinder personal growth and success. When anger takes control, it not only clouds one's judgment but also robs a person of their potential for greatness. Many individuals, in moments of rage, say or do things they later regret, leading to broken relationships, missed opportunities, and self-inflicted obstacles.

Anger, when left unchecked, acts like wildfire, spreading negativity and causing pain—not just to others but also to oneself. It disrupts inner peace, fuels impulsive actions, and creates unnecessary conflict, making it difficult to achieve one's goals. A person consumed by anger often finds themselves entangled in problems that could have been avoided with patience and rational thinking.

The significance of self-control and the immense power that lies in patience. True strength does not come from reacting aggressively but from maintaining composure in difficult situations. Those who master their temper are better equipped to make wise decisions, handle adversity with grace, and build meaningful relationships based on understanding and respect.

By promoting the virtue of patience, individuals should embrace calmness as a tool for personal and professional success. A peaceful mind is not only free from the burdens of regret and resentment but also capable of navigating life's challenges with clarity and wisdom. In essence, emotional balance is key to a fulfilling and prosperous life.

A young man, known for his temper, was constantly in conflict with those around him. His anger would flare up over trivial matters, leaving him with deep regrets. One day, after yet another heated argument, he came across a simple yet profound realization: Anger is a thief, stealing away potential. This thought lingered in his mind, urging him to reflect on his actions.

Determined to change, he began practicing patience, learning to pause before reacting. At first, it was difficult, but with time, he noticed a shift—his mind became clearer, his relationships improved, and he no longer carried the weight of regret. As he embraced calmness, he found himself making wiser choices, achieving his goals with greater ease, and discovering that true strength lay not in anger, but in self-control.

The Danger of Anger

Alexander the Great, one of history's most successful and revered conquerors, experienced a moment of tragic impulsivity that would haunt him for the rest of his life.

During a banquet in 328 BC, Alexander, drunk and enraged by a disagreement, killed his close friend and officer, Cleitus the Black. Cleitus had once saved Alexander's life during battle, and the two had been comrades for many years. Yet, in that moment of unchecked anger, Alexander's fury clouded his judgment, leading him to take the life of someone he deeply respected. The aftermath was devastating for Alexander. His remorse and guilt were overwhelming, and he spent days in mourning for the loss of his friend. This incident underscores the dangers of uncontrolled anger, even for the greatest of individuals. It serves as a reminder that anger, when allowed to dictate actions, can erase years of trust and friendship, leaving behind regret and irreversible consequences. Alexander, who had the world at his feet, was brought low by a moment of rage. The story of his impulsive act and its tragic aftermath warns us of the destructive power of anger and the importance of emotional control, no matter one's stature or achievements.

"Patience is not the ability to wait, but the ability to keep a good attitude while waiting."

A drop of lemon spoils pure milk,
Greed taints knowledge, smooth as silk.
Such is the nature of poison's ilk,
For ambition's stain dims virtue's silk.

Greed and Its Effects

Just as a single drop of lemon juice can curdle a pot of pure milk, a trace of unchecked ambition can corrupt something that was once pure and valuable. Ambition, when balanced with wisdom and ethics, can drive a person toward greatness. However, when fueled by greed and selfishness, it has the power to taint even the noblest qualities, such as knowledge, virtue, and integrity, turning them into tools for personal gain rather than collective good.

Greed and ambition often begin subtly, creeping in under the guise of motivation and determination. Yet, when left unchecked, they can consume a person's moral compass, blinding them to the ethical consequences of their actions. History is filled with examples of individuals who once stood for righteousness but, driven by an insatiable hunger for power, wealth, or recognition, ultimately compromised their values.

Much like spoiled milk, which loses its nourishing quality and becomes unfit for consumption, a person corrupted by ambition loses the essence of their true self. Their achievements, instead of being sources of pride and inspiration, become symbols of misplaced priorities. True success does not lie in reaching the top at any cost, but in preserving one's integrity and using ambition as a force for good rather than destruction.

Therefore, it is crucial to maintain a balance, to temper ambition with humility, and to ensure that our desires do not overshadow our values. A life driven by pure intentions remains untainted, just as milk retains its purity when free from contamination.

There once was a young man, gifted with intelligence and driven by an insatiable thirst for knowledge. Eager to master the depths of wisdom, he sought guidance from a reclusive yet revered hermit who lived atop a serene mountain. Under the hermit's tutelage, the young man absorbed the teachings of philosophy, morality, and the art of self-discipline. He practiced humility, believing that wisdom was a path to enlightenment, not mere achievement.

However, as time passed, his knowledge brought him admiration from those around him. People began to praise his intellect, and whispers of his brilliance spread far and wide. Slowly, his once-pure pursuit of wisdom turned into a craving for recognition. He found himself speaking not to enlighten but to impress. He sought authority over others, believing that his knowledge entitled him to a higher status. His humility began to fade, replaced by pride and an unquenchable thirst for power.

Sensing this shift, the hermit invited the young man to sit with him one evening. Without a word, he poured a bowl of fresh, pure milk and let it sit before them. Then, with deliberate precision, he took a single drop of lemon juice and let it fall into the milk. Almost instantly, the milk curdled and turned sour. The young man watched in surprise as the smooth, nourishing liquid transformed into something spoiled and unfit to drink.

The hermit finally spoke. "This is what happens when greed taints wisdom," he said. "Milk, like knowledge, is pure and nourishing. But a single drop of selfish ambition—unchecked and unbalanced—can ruin it entirely. Power and recognition may come, but if they overshadow humility, they will turn wisdom into arrogance and virtue into vanity."

The young man sat in silence, realization dawning upon him. He saw how his hunger for recognition had eroded the very foundation of what he had once sought. With a humbled heart, he vowed to restore the purity of his intentions, understanding that true wisdom is not measured by admiration or status but by the ability to remain humble despite possessing great knowledge.

Greed Corrupts Knowledge

The 2008 Financial Crisis stands as one of the most significant global economic disasters in modern history. At its core, the crisis was driven by the greed of financial institutions and experts who, in their pursuit of ever-increasing profits, ignored the risks associated with subprime mortgages and unsustainable lending practices. Investment banks, mortgage lenders, and insurance companies all played a part in creating a bubble, and when the housing market collapsed, the entire financial system was exposed as fragile and corrupt. The very knowledge and expertise that these institutions relied on to make sound financial decisions were tainted by greed. Instead of using their understanding of economics and finance to protect the system and serve the public good, they used it to create increasingly risky financial products and schemes.

The crisis showed how knowledge, when driven by selfish motives and a desire for wealth, can lose its integrity and lead to disastrous consequences. What was once seen as a mark of expertise turned into a mechanism for exploitation, demonstrating that when greed takes precedence, wisdom and judgment are easily compromised. The 2008 Financial Crisis is a stark reminder that unchecked greed can corrupt the most sophisticated of financial systems.

"Greed, like fire, consumes everything in its path."

The tongue seeks taste to fill its days,
Husband and wife long for children's praise,
And fire consumes all it surveys,
For desires, unchecked, lead hearts astray.

The Consequences of Unchecked Desires

Desires, when unchecked, can easily lead people astray. The tongue seeks to indulge in pleasures, the heart desires praise and recognition, and fire consumes everything in its path. However, these unchecked desires, if not kept in balance, often result in disappointment, conflict, and loss. It's important to control one's desires and keep them in check to live a balanced and fulfilling life. Excessive longing for anything can cloud judgment and lead to chaos.

In a small village, there lived a man who was constantly seeking approval from others. He wanted wealth, fame, and admiration, but his desires grew unchecked. He worked day and night, trying to acquire more, but as he gained wealth, he lost his peace. His home was filled with restlessness, and no matter how much he obtained, he never felt content. One day, an old wise woman told him, "Desires, like a fire, will consume you if you feed them endlessly. Learn to control them, and you will find peace." He finally came to know that true contentment lay in moderation, not in endless pursuit.

Insatiable Desires

The California Gold Rush of 1848-1855 serves as a cautionary tale of how insatiable desires for wealth can lead to unforeseen consequences. When gold was discovered at Sutter's Mill in California, thousands of prospectors flooded the region, driven by the hope of striking it rich. The promise of gold lured people from all walks of life, sparking a rush of immigration and settlement. However, this insatiable greed had devastating effects on both the environment and society. The influx of miners and settlers led to the destruction of landscapes, deforestation, and contamination of rivers with mercury. Society became increasingly divided, as miners competed ruthlessly for resources, and lawlessness ensued in the absence of proper governance. The Gold Rush also exacerbated the mistreatment of indigenous populations, who were displaced and exploited in the search for wealth. The insatiable desire for gold proved that unchecked ambition can result in environmental degradation and societal instability. The Gold Rush serves as a reminder of how unchecked desires—

especially when driven by greed—can have lasting, destructive effects on both people and the planet.

"Desires unfulfilled are like fire—never satisfied, always consuming."

Chapter 14

Practice and Dedication

Success is not achieved through talent alone but through consistent effort and dedication. Practice refines skills, turning potential into mastery. Every great achievement is the result of perseverance, where failure becomes a lesson rather than a setback. Dedication demands discipline, patience, and a willingness to improve. Without persistent effort, even the most gifted individuals remain stagnant. Growth is a continuous journey, and true progress comes to those who commit to learning and improvement. Whether in art, work, or personal growth, dedication is the key that unlocks excellence. Mastery is the result of relentless practice. Da Vinci, Beethoven, and Einstein exemplify that genius is built through dedication, not mere talent. History rewards those who persevere beyond failure.

What is practice worth without devotion's flame?
What is a recipe without pure intention's aim?
What is worship without dedication's steady motion?
A hollow vessel echoes, devoid of true emotion.

Devotion in Practice

Devotion is the very essence that gives life and meaning to any action. It is the invisible force that turns routine practices into heartfelt expressions, elevating them from mere obligations to profound experiences. Without devotion, even the most sacred rituals become mechanical, devoid of purpose and true significance. A prayer uttered without feeling is but a string of empty words, just as a task performed without passion becomes a mundane duty rather than an act of fulfillment.

Just as a flame fuels a lamp, spreading warmth and light, devotion ignites the purpose behind our worship, work, and learning. It is not the grandeur of the ritual that matters, but the sincerity behind it. A dish prepared with the finest ingredients may still lack flavor if made without love, while a simple meal cooked with care and affection can nourish not only the body but also the soul. Likewise, a hollow vessel may appear whole, but it remains empty inside, unable to hold meaning or substance.

True devotion breathes life into everything we do. Whether in prayer, in the pursuit of knowledge, or in the smallest of daily tasks, it transforms ordinary actions into something extraordinary. It bridges the gap between effort and fulfillment, between action and impact. When we act with sincerity and devotion, our work resonates with deeper meaning, touching hearts and connecting us to a higher purpose.

In the end, devotion is not just about performing an action—it is about infusing that action with soul, turning the ordinary into the divine, and making every effort count in ways beyond the tangible.

Arjun was once known for his breathtaking paintings, each brushstroke infused with passion and soul. His art spoke to people, evoking deep emotions and admiration. However, as his reputation grew, so did the demands on his time. Faced with tight deadlines and mounting expectations, he began painting with speed rather than heart. His hands moved skillfully, producing works that were technically flawless, yet something was missing—the essence that once made his art truly special.

One day, a wealthy patron visited his gallery and studied his latest pieces. The colors were rich, the details immaculate, yet the paintings failed to stir any feeling. After a long pause, the patron turned to Arjun and remarked, "Your paintings feel like empty vessels—beautiful, but without spirit. They no longer whisper stories or breathe life as they once did."

Arjun was taken aback. He had been so focused on efficiency and perfection that he hadn't noticed the subtle yet profound loss in his work. That night, he sat in his studio, staring at a half-finished canvas, reflecting on the words of the patron. He remembered the joy he once felt in creating art—not for recognition, not for sales, but for the sheer love of expression.

Determined to reclaim that passion, Arjun slowed down. He let his brush dance freely, not to meet a deadline, but to capture the emotions he had long ignored. He painted with devotion, pouring his heart into each stroke, reliving the magic that once defined his artistry. As days passed, his paintings transformed.

They no longer just pleased the eye; they touched the soul. Viewers once again felt the depth and emotion in his work, and admiration returned—not just for his skill, but for the life he breathed into his creations.

In that journey of rediscovery, Arjun learned a valuable truth: true artistry is not just about technique or perfection—it is about the passion, devotion, and soul infused into the work.

Thomas Edison's journey to inventing the light bulb was anything but smooth. Imagine facing failure not once, not twice, but over a thousand times. For most, such repeated setbacks would be enough to abandon the dream, convinced that success was impossible. But not Edison. He saw failure not as defeat, but as discovery. When asked about his countless unsuccessful attempts, he famously remarked, "I have not failed. I've just found 10,000 ways that won't work."

Edison's unwavering determination turned obstacles into stepping stones. Every experiment, every misstep, was a lesson bringing him closer to his breakthrough. While the world saw failure, he saw progress. His story is a powerful reminder that great achievements are not born out of luck or overnight success, but through relentless practice, tireless refinement, and an unshakable commitment to one's vision.

Today, every time we flick on a light switch, we unknowingly pay homage to Edison's perseverance. His invention illuminates not just our homes, but the very essence of resilience—the idea that failure is not the end of the road, but a crucial part of the journey to greatness. For anyone feeling disheartened by setbacks, Edison's life offers a timeless whisper of encouragement: "Keep going. Every failure brings you one step closer to your moment of brilliance."

"What is done with heart is always done well."

Repetition hones the song's tone.
Even neem tastes sweet when practice is known.
With effort, fruits of labor are shown,
And perseverance makes the seedling grown.

The Fruits of Repetition and Perseverance

Repetition and practice are the chisels that sculpt even the most formidable challenges, transforming the impossible into the achievable. Like the steady drip of water that carves through stone, perseverance wears down obstacles and paves the way for success. Consider the neem leaf—its bitterness at first may seem unpalatable, yet with time, persistence, and adaptation, even its taste can become tolerable, if not beneficial. Similarly, hard work refines raw effort, turning initial struggles into stepping stones toward mastery.

Much like a seedling requires nourishment, care, and patience to grow into a flourishing tree, every small effort contributes to progress. Each challenge overcome, each failure endured, and each lesson learned adds another ring to the tree of wisdom and resilience. Growth is never instantaneous—it demands unwavering commitment, repeated trials, and the courage to push forward despite setbacks.

Diligence, though demanding and often exhausting, bears the sweetest rewards. A farmer toiling under the scorching sun does not reap his harvest overnight, nor does an artist achieve brilliance without countless strokes of the brush. Similarly, no skill is mastered, no knowledge is deepened, and no dream is realized without the continuous force of perseverance.

In a world that often seeks instant gratification, it is easy to underestimate the power of sustained effort. Yet history has shown that the greatest minds, the most celebrated innovators, and the most inspiring leaders all have one thing in common: persistence. Their achievements are not products of mere talent but of relentless practice, refinement, and the refusal to surrender to failure.

Nothing of true value is ever attained without persistence, for practice is the foundation of all progress. It is the bridge that connects potential to greatness, effort to excellence, and dreams to reality. Those who embrace perseverance as a lifelong companion will find that no goal is too distant, no challenge too daunting, and no aspiration beyond reach.

The Potter's Mastery: A Tale of Perseverance

In a small village, there lived a young man named Rohan who wished to become a master potter. Inspired by the intricate designs and flawless symmetry of the pots crafted by an old village potter, he eagerly approached the artisan, pleading to become his apprentice.

The old potter, with a knowing smile, handed Rohan a lump of clay and instructed him to shape a simple pot. Excited, Rohan began molding the clay, but each time he tried, the pot either cracked, collapsed, or turned out lopsided. Frustrated, he looked up at the potter and said, "It seems impossible! My hands are just not meant for this."

The potter chuckled and placed a perfectly crafted pot before him. "Do you think I shaped this on my first attempt?" he asked. "Every masterpiece begins as a formless lump. Only through repetition, patience, and learning from failures does it take shape."

Encouraged by the potter's wisdom, Rohan decided not to give up. Day after day, he practiced, failing countless times but improving with each mistake. His fingers, once clumsy, learned the delicate balance of pressure and precision. His eyes, once filled with doubt, began to see possibilities in every flaw. Months turned into years, and soon, Rohan was shaping exquisite pots with effortless grace.

One day, the potter declared, "You have mastered the craft." Rohan, now a skilled artisan himself, looked at his creations and realized that the secret to success had never been talent alone—it was perseverance, the unwavering commitment to practice despite failures.

From then on, whenever a new apprentice complained of difficulty, Rohan would simply smile and say, "Every pot starts as a misshapen lump. Keep shaping, and soon, you'll craft your own masterpiece."

Ludwig van Beethoven, one of history's greatest composers, faced an unimaginable trial—progressive and irreversible deafness. For a musician whose life revolved around sound, this affliction seemed like a cruel twist of fate, a barrier that could have silenced his genius forever. Yet, Beethoven refused to surrender to despair. Rather than allowing his condition to define him, he turned his greatest adversity into a force of creative defiance.

As his hearing deteriorated, he adapted. He relied on vibrations, feeling the music through his fingers against the piano, visualizing each note with an internal clarity that transcended the physical realm. Through relentless practice and an unyielding devotion to his art, he continued composing, crafting some of the most profound and enduring pieces in musical history.

His Fifth Symphony, often interpreted as a musical representation of fate knocking at the door, embodies the struggles he faced, while his Moonlight Sonata whispers the melancholy of his silent world. But perhaps his most awe-inspiring achievement came when he composed the Ninth Symphony, a masterpiece of unparalleled depth and emotion—despite being completely deaf. When it premiered, Beethoven stood on stage, unable to hear the thunderous applause of the audience. It was only when a musician gently turned him toward the crowd that he saw the overwhelming admiration his work had evoked.

Beethoven's story is not just one of musical brilliance—it is a testament to the power of resilience, passion, and unwavering determination. It proves that true greatness is not shaped by circumstances but by the will to persevere. His journey reminds us that obstacles, no matter how insurmountable they seem, are often the very trials that forge our path to success. Through dedication, belief, and an unbreakable spirit, even the greatest challenges can become stepping stones to extraordinary achievements. Beethoven's legacy continues to inspire, echoing through time as a resounding anthem of human perseverance and triumph.

"Practice makes perfect."

Saintly robes may veil the mind,
Restless thoughts, chaos unconfined.
Does hitting an anthill slay the serpent behind?
For true peace lies in the quiet of the mind.

True Peace Comes from a Quiet Mind

Mental tranquility is the cornerstone of true peace, a state that cannot be attained merely through external appearances or superficial symbols of spirituality. Donning saintly robes or adopting an air of serenity may give the illusion of inner harmony, but true peace is not something that can be worn—it must be cultivated from within. A restless mind, filled with turbulent thoughts and unresolved conflicts, will remain in turmoil, no matter how calm and composed one appears on the surface.

True inner peace is not about escaping reality or suppressing emotions but about achieving a state of clarity and balance. It is about quieting the storms within, untangling the knots of anxiety, and finding a deep-rooted sense of contentment that is not swayed by external chaos. Just as hitting an anthill in search of a serpent is a futile effort—because the true source of the danger lies deeper—attempting to achieve peace by focusing on outward distractions fails to address the core issues of inner unrest.

Genuine peace arises from self-awareness, self-discipline, and the ability to let go of negative emotions that weigh heavily on the mind. It comes from understanding that external circumstances are ever-changing, but the mind has the power to remain steady amidst the shifting tides of life. The pursuit of true tranquility is an inward journey, one that requires reflection, mindfulness, and the courage to confront the deeper layers of one's own being.

Only when the mind is free from unnecessary worries, grudges, and fears can one experience a profound and lasting peace. It is not found in fleeting pleasures or temporary distractions but in the deep stillness that comes from embracing life with wisdom, acceptance, and inner harmony.

The Silent Monk and the Restless King

In an ancient kingdom, there lived a mighty king named Rajendra, whose wealth and power were unmatched. Yet, despite having everything, he was plagued by a restless mind. His nights were sleepless, his thoughts raced like untamed horses, and no amount of luxury could bring him peace.

One day, Rajendra heard of a revered monk who lived in the mountains, known for his extraordinary calmness. Hoping to find the secret to inner peace, the king set off on a journey to meet him.

Upon reaching the mountain, he found the monk seated beneath a great banyan tree, dressed in simple robes, his eyes reflecting a profound stillness. The king bowed and said, "Master, I have everything—power, wealth, and comfort—yet my mind is never at rest. Teach me the secret to true peace."

The monk smiled and handed the king a cup, filling it to the brim with water. Then, without warning, he continued pouring until the water spilled over, drenching the king's hands.

"Why did you do that?" the king asked, startled.

The monk replied, "Your mind is like this cup—filled to the top with worries, desires, and distractions. No matter how much you seek peace, there is no space for it to enter. True tranquility comes when you empty the unnecessary."

The king pondered these words, but he was still unconvinced. "But I have seen many who appear peaceful—sages in saffron robes, priests in temples. They seem at ease. Should I renounce my kingdom and live like them?"

The monk picked up a stone and threw it into the nearby lake. Ripples disturbed the water, spreading outward in restless waves. "A calm lake reflects the sky perfectly, but the slightest disturbance distorts its image. Peace is not about robes or appearances. Even in a palace, a quiet mind remains undisturbed, while in a forest, a restless mind is still chaotic."

The king remained silent, absorbing the lesson. He realized that true peace wasn't about changing his surroundings but about mastering his mind. From that day forward, he practiced mindfulness, learned to let go of unnecessary burdens, and gradually, his inner storms began to settle.

Years later, he ruled with wisdom, not just power. His people no longer saw him as just a king, but as a man who had discovered something far greater—an unshakable inner peace.

The mind is everything. What you think, you become

Swami Vivekananda, one of India's most revered spiritual leaders, was known for his wisdom and ability to inspire others. However, even he faced moments of inner struggle. As a monk dedicated to spiritual enlightenment, Vivekananda acknowledged that mastering one's mind was a continuous challenge. Despite his public persona as a serene and enlightened figure, he struggled with worldly distractions and doubts. These moments of mental restlessness are a testament to the universal nature of the human condition.

Even the most spiritually advanced individuals must engage in constant self-reflection and discipline to control the mind. Vivekananda's teachings emphasized the importance of self-control, meditation, and mindfulness in achieving spiritual liberation. His admission of personal struggles with distractions highlights the reality that inner peace is not easily attained, even by those who devote their lives to it. His example encourages us to be patient with ourselves and to recognize that the journey to mastering the mind is a lifelong process, one that requires dedication, practice, and perseverance.

"Peace comes from within. Do not seek it without."

Endurance and Practice

Helen Keller's life was a testament to the power of perseverance. Deaf and blind from infancy due to an illness, her world seemed shrouded in silence and darkness. Yet, with the guidance of her dedicated teacher, Anne Sullivan, Helen embarked on an extraordinary journey to communicate and learn.

Through relentless practice, Helen learned to spell words into her hand, connecting the sensation to objects in the world. Later, she mastered Braille and even learned to speak. Helen's determination didn't stop there—she became a renowned author, activist, and speaker, inspiring millions.

Her story is a reminder that persistence can overcome even the most daunting obstacles. With dedication and support, what seems impossible can become achievable. Helen Keller's life encourages us to pursue our goals with unwavering determination.

Chapter 15

Leadership and Influence

Leadership is not about control but about guidance and inspiration. True leaders influence through example, not authority. They uplift others, create vision, and foster unity. A leader's impact is not measured by power but by the lives, they touch. Influence comes from wisdom, integrity, and the ability to understand people. Leadership requires responsibility, as actions affect many. While some lead with force, true leadership is built on trust and respect. The best leaders listen, adapt, and serve with purpose, leaving a legacy that extends beyond their time. True leaders, from Julius Caesar to Nelson Mandela, shape history. While some rule through fear, others inspire through vision. Influence is not about power alone but about leaving a legacy that endures.

The worm at the root ends the tree's timeless story.
The worm on the branch dims its radiant glory.
The wicked heart destroys the righteous wholly,
A truth as old as life's narrative, grim and holy.

The Root of Evil

A tree's demise begins with a worm at its root, just as moral decay starts subtly, often unnoticed. A branch attacked by a worm loses its beauty, just as a wicked heart taints an individual's character. Whether it is a person, family, or society, destruction often arises from within. Small acts of neglect or malice can snowball into irreversible damage. The poem serves as a reminder to nurture integrity and root out negativity before it spreads. Just as a tree needs care to thrive, so do our values require vigilance to withstand life's trials.

A prosperous farmer noticed a small worm on his apple tree but ignored it, thinking it harmless. Over time, the worm multiplied, infecting the roots and branches until the tree bore no fruit and withered. Meanwhile, his neighbor regularly inspected his trees, removing pests at the first sign. When the farmer sought advice, his neighbor remarked, "Neglect lets destruction take root." Realizing his mistake, the farmer vowed to nurture his trees and his character with equal care.

In the early 1970s, the Watergate Scandal unraveled a web of corruption in the highest office of the United States. What started as a seemingly small act—spying on political opponents—quickly escalated into a full-blown crisis, leading to the resignation of President Richard Nixon. The scandal revealed how the actions of a few, driven by greed and a hunger for power, can poison an entire institution.

This incident serves as a stark reminder: corruption doesn't start big. It begins as a tiny worm gnawing at the root of integrity. Left unchecked, it spreads, causing the collapse of the strongest trees. The Watergate Scandal taught the world the importance of ethical leadership and accountability. It's a cautionary tale that warns us to guard against the small lapses that could grow into catastrophic failures. Integrity, like a tree's roots, must be nurtured and protected. Without it, even the mightiest fall.

"Evil begins as a seed but grows into a forest."

Put the petty in power, and virtue departs,
A dog biting shoes knows not sugar's part.
Mean men misrule with ignorant hearts,
For virtue is lost where selfishness starts.

Unworthy Leadership

When those who lack virtue are given power, they misuse it, leading to the decline of moral values. The "dog biting shoes" metaphor suggests that small-minded, ignorant individuals are unable to understand the value of kindness or virtue. Their actions harm society because they fail to recognize the importance of selflessness. True virtue is absent where selfishness and ignorance prevail, and the power wielded by such individuals only exacerbates the loss of righteousness in their domain.

In a small kingdom, the ruler was kind and just, but when he was overthrown, a greedy and cruel man took his place. This new leader was selfish and only cared about his own gain. The people, once happy and prosperous, soon suffered under his rule. A wise elder advised, "When selfishness leads, virtue flees." Eventually, the people revolted and restored the old ruler, realizing that power, when held by mean-spirited men, only brings harm. They learned that virtue must lead, not selfishness, for only then can a nation thrive.

Emperor Nero of Rome, infamous for his indulgence and self-absorption, embodies the chaos caused by ineffective leadership. His reign was marked by extravagance, disregard for the welfare of his people, and alleged involvement in the burning of Rome in 64 AD, during which he infamously played music as the city burned. Nero's leadership failed to address the needs of his citizens and led Rome into turmoil.

His reign serves as a stark warning about the dangers of placing unfit individuals in positions of power. Nero's selfishness and lack of empathy not only tarnished his legacy but caused harm to the empire he ruled.

This story is a timeless lesson that leadership must be guided by wisdom, compassion, and a genuine sense of responsibility. Without these qualities, leadership breeds division and destruction. Nero's downfall underscores the importance of having leaders who serve the people, not their own desires.

"Power corrupts, and absolute power corrupts absolutely."

If the king's a monkey, the minister's a pig,
Commanders are birds, soldiers, ants big.
Rats and cats replace horses in this gig,
For wisdom falls where corruption digs.

Corruption Destroys Wisdom

When corruption usurps wisdom, disorder spreads like wildfire, dismantling the fabric of society. Those entrusted with power, if driven by greed and deceit, sow destruction instead of prosperity, leading the land into ruin. When integrity is cast aside, wisdom withers, leaving behind a world where chaos reigns unchecked. True leadership is not measured by authority alone but by the ability to nurture justice, uphold virtue, and guide with wisdom. A society bereft of such leadership is doomed to collapse, for without wisdom, even the strongest foundations crumble into dust.

A kingdom once thrived under a wise king who cared for his people. However, over time, the king's ministers became corrupt, and his advisers were more interested in their own wealth than in the welfare of the people. The kingdom slowly began to crumble under poor leadership. The king, blinded by his own power, failed to notice how the wise counsel had been replaced by sycophants. One day, a wise sage entered the kingdom and pointed out that the kingdom had become like a palace ruled by a monkey and a pig. The king realized that true wisdom had been abandoned for greed. He sought to restore wisdom, but by then, the damage was irreversible.

Foolish Leadership

The fall of the Qing Dynasty in China was a direct result of foolish leadership and mismanagement during the late 19th and early 20th centuries. Empress Dowager Cixi, who held power in the imperial court for much of the late Qing period, is often blamed for the dynasty's collapse. Her rule, marked by self-interest and authoritarian control, failed to modernize China in the face of growing Western influence and internal rebellion. Cixi's reliance on inept officials, as well as her inability to recognize the need for reform, left China vulnerable to foreign domination and internal strife. The Boxer Rebellion, the First Sino-Japanese War, and widespread unrest underscored the failure of the Qing leadership to respond to the changing dynamics of the world. The Empress's leadership style, which focused more on maintaining personal power than on addressing the needs of the country, ultimately led to the dynasty's downfall. The collapse of the Qing Dynasty serves as a cautionary tale about the dangers of foolish leadership. It highlights how leaders who fail to adapt to the challenges of their time—either through incompetence or hubris—can bring about the ruin of entire nations.

"When the blind lead the blind, both fall into the pit."

Chapter 16

Appearance and Reality

Things are not always as they seem. Appearance can be deceiving, while truth often lies beneath the surface. Many are misled by outward impressions, failing to look deeper. Reality requires perception beyond what is immediately visible. True understanding comes from questioning, observing, and seeking clarity. While appearances may be manipulated, reality remains unchanged. Those who rely on superficial judgments often misinterpret situations, while those who seek deeper insight uncover the truth. Wisdom lies in recognizing that reality is more complex than what meets the eye. History teaches us that things are rarely as they seem. The deceptive peace before World War I or the hidden agendas of rulers show that wisdom lies in discerning the truth behind appearances.

The pepper seed, black and small, conceals its heat,
Its power revealed when bitten to eat.
The strength of saints is quiet yet elite,
Their influence humble, yet pure and complete.

The Hidden Power of Quiet Strength

True power often resides in the unassuming, much like the tiny pepper seed that holds intense heat within. Those with genuine wisdom and virtue move through the world with quiet strength, leaving a profound impact without seeking recognition. Their influence is not in grand declarations but in the depth of their actions, shaping lives with humility and grace. Just as the pepper's potency is only revealed upon tasting, the true strength of noble souls is felt in the transformations they inspire. In a world drawn to outward displays of power, it is the silent resilience of wisdom that endures and uplifts.

A quiet teacher in a bustling city worked tirelessly to uplift underprivileged children. Though he rarely sought recognition, his students grew into compassionate leaders, spreading the values he taught. Years later, at a grand event, one of his students credited their success to his silent yet profound guidance. The teacher's humility and quiet power had shaped countless lives, proving that true greatness lies in quiet influence.

Alan Turing, a quiet and unassuming mathematician, played an instrumental role in World War II. Working at Bletchley Park, Turing developed the Bombe, a machine that decoded messages encrypted by the Nazi Enigma machine. This breakthrough gave the Allies a decisive advantage, shortening the war by years and saving countless lives.

Despite his monumental contributions, Turing's work remained classified for decades, and he faced persecution for his personal life. Yet, his quiet brilliance reshaped the world, laying the foundations for modern computing.

Turing's story highlights the power of hidden strength. Like the subtle heat of pepper that surprises the tongue, his genius operated quietly but had a profound impact. His life inspires us to recognize the value of unseen efforts and the transformative power of intellect and determination.

"True strength is silent."

Though black in hue, Kasturi spreads its scent,
Its fragrance graces all where it's sent.
So masters guard their power, unbent,
Their influence silent, yet heaven-sent.

The Silent Power of Grace

Like the unassuming Kasturi, whose rich fragrance permeates the air, true wisdom and greatness manifest not through grand displays but through quiet, far-reaching influence. Those who possess deep insight and virtue do not seek recognition, yet their presence shapes the world in profound ways. Their strength lies not in outward appearance but in the purity of their essence, leaving an enduring mark through their wisdom and grace. True impact is not measured by noise or display but by the silent transformation it brings to those who encounter it.

A humble gardener cared for his village's neglected garden, planting fragrant flowers. Though no one noticed his work at first, the garden began to bloom, and its scent attracted visitors from far and wide. When asked who had created such beauty, the gardener smiled and said, "The flowers speak for themselves." His silent efforts brought joy and unity to the village, demonstrating that quiet grace can create profound change.

Mahatma Gandhi, a man of frail appearance and simple demeanor, changed the course of history with his philosophy of nonviolent resistance. In India's struggle for independence, Gandhi didn't lead with force or loud declarations; instead, he inspired through quiet action and steadfast principles. His salt march, fasting, and peaceful protests captivated millions, demonstrating the power of inner strength over brute force.

Gandhi's influence spread like the scent of Kasturi, subtle yet transformative. It reached people of all classes and creeds, uniting them under the banner of justice. Even global leaders like Martin Luther King Jr. and Nelson Mandela drew inspiration from his methods. His life serves as a testament to the profound impact of humility, resolve, and moral clarity.

The legacy of Gandhi reminds us that true masters don't dominate—they empower others to discover their own strength. His influence continues to guide movements for justice and peace worldwide, proving that leadership rooted in virtue creates change that transcends time.

"Grace needs no proclamation."

Dirty clothes and unkempt hair disgrace,
Even a noble-born loses face.
Appearances matter in every place,
For they reflect the heart's hidden trace.

Letting appearances and Integrity

One's outward appearance is often a silent testament to the state of the inner self. Neglect in attire and grooming can obscure even the noblest of virtues, casting a shadow on one's dignity and self-respect. True refinement is not about vanity but about presenting oneself as a reflection of inner discipline, harmony, and self-worth. The way we carry ourselves speaks before words ever do, revealing our values, mindfulness, and regard for the world. Just as a pristine mirror reflects a clear image, our external presence subtly echoes the depth of our character and the integrity of our soul.

A king, proud of his lineage, wore the finest robes and sat on a magnificent throne. One day, a poor traveler entered his court, dressed in simple, tattered clothes. The people of the kingdom sneered at the traveler, but the king invited him to speak. The traveler, though humble in appearance, spoke wisdom that moved the entire court. The king realized that outward appearances should not define one's worth, and that true nobility comes from within. He began to take care of both his heart and his image, teaching his people that inner integrity should be reflected in one's outer presentation.

Outward Appearance

Before Abraham Lincoln became the revered president of the United States, he was often dismissed by others due to his modest clothing and unkempt appearance. Many overlooked the depth of his wisdom and leadership potential, focusing instead on his outward appearance. It was only later, as his ideas and actions spoke louder than his physical presence, that people began to recognize his true worth.

Lincoln's early career underscores the danger of judging people based on superficial qualities. His life reminds us that wisdom, character, and leadership are not always reflected in one's appearance. In a world where first impressions can be deceiving, Lincoln's rise from obscurity serves as a powerful reminder that what matters most is what lies beneath the surface. The story of his journey emphasizes that true value is often hidden from view and requires deeper understanding to be recognized.

"You never get a second chance to make a first impression."

Wearing saintly garb, shaving the head,
Their souls remain unclean instead.
Virtue lies not in how one's dressed,
But in actions, where true grace is blessed.

True Virtue is in Actions

Virtue is not measured by outward symbols or ritualistic displays but by the depth of one's actions and character. Merely adorning saintly robes or adopting external signs of holiness does not bestow goodness; true righteousness stems from inner purity and is reflected in deeds, not appearances. Genuine grace is revealed through integrity, kindness, and selfless actions, shaping a life of true meaning. It is not the attire one wears but the virtues one embodies that define greatness, urging us to cultivate sincerity and wisdom over superficial impressions.

A man was known in his village for wearing robes of a saint, and he often shaved his head to appear pious. People would bow before him, thinking him to be holy. However, his actions did not reflect the purity he projected. He was rude to his neighbors and greedy in his dealings. One day, a poor traveler entered the village and, despite having nothing, showed great kindness and humility. The villagers soon realized that virtue lies not in outward appearances but in how one treats others. The man in robes could not fool them any longer, and they learned that true holiness is shown in deeds, not dress.

False Appearances

The Salem Witch Trials of 1692 were a dark period in American history, marked by fear, superstition, and mass hysteria. Hundreds of individuals, mostly women, were accused of practicing witchcraft based on little to no evidence. Instead, many of the accusations were rooted in the outward behavior or appearance of the accused, rather than any tangible proof of wrongdoing. A person who acted strangely, or was socially outcast, might be seen as a witch simply because they didn't conform to societal expectations. In a particularly cruel irony, the trials were fueled by the very notion of appearances—those who acted "properly" were often believed to be innocent, while those who deviated from the norm were condemned. The witch trials highlight the dangers of judging people based on superficial traits or behavior, without seeking deeper truths. In the rush to find scapegoats for societal fears, many innocent lives were destroyed. The Salem Witch Trials serve as a stark reminder of how dangerous it is to rely on false appearances and assumptions. In the end, they demonstrate how easily a community can be led astray when fear and prejudice are allowed to overshadow reason and justice.

"A promise is only as strong as the effort behind it."

Chapter 17

Change and Impermanence

Change is the only constant in life. Everything evolves—thoughts, circumstances, and experiences. Resistance to change leads to suffering, while acceptance brings growth. Nothing remains forever, and impermanence teaches the value of the present moment. Those who adapt find success, while those who cling to the past struggle. Growth requires embracing change, knowing that endings create new beginnings. Life is a journey of transformation, where letting go allows space for new possibilities. Understanding impermanence fosters wisdom, gratitude, and the ability to move forward with resilience. Empires crumble, ideologies shift, and history evolves. From the fall of Byzantium to the digital revolution, change is inevitable. Adapting with wisdom ensures survival, while resistance to change leads to downfall.

Men blind to truth refuse to see,
The greatness of those who've ceased to be.
The past shines brighter than their decree,
For in history's shadows, truth runs free.

The Eternal Truth of the Past

Wisdom is etched in the annals of history, yet many fail to recognize its enduring light. The fleeting opinions of the present often pale in comparison to the timeless truths left behind by great minds of the past. While the world rushes forward, dismissing history's value, its lessons remain steadfast, offering clarity to those who seek them. True understanding comes not from ignoring the past but from embracing its wisdom with humility. The echoes of history are not mere relics—they are guiding beacons, illuminating the path for those wise enough to listen.

A young ruler dismissed his ancestors' wisdom, insisting his methods were superior. One day, a drought struck the kingdom, and his strategies failed. Desperate, he studied old records and found a method devised by his forefathers to conserve water. Following their guidance, he saved his kingdom and realized the importance of respecting history. From then on, he taught his people to honor the past, understanding that wisdom often hides in history's folds.

Nikola Tesla, one of history's most brilliant inventors, envisioned a world powered by wireless electricity, clean energy, and groundbreaking technologies. Despite his revolutionary ideas, Tesla was overshadowed during his lifetime by figures like Thomas Edison, who often prioritized profit over innovation.

Tesla's genius was undervalued, and he died impoverished, his contributions largely ignored. Yet, his inventions, such as alternating current (AC), laid the foundation for modern electrical systems. It was only after his death that the world began to recognize his brilliance, honoring him as a visionary far ahead of his time.

Tesla's story highlights humanity's tendency to overlook living geniuses while glorifying them posthumously. It reminds us to value innovation and creativity in the present, lest we miss out on transformative ideas. His life serves as a cautionary tale about the importance of recognizing contemporary brilliance before it's too late.

"History is the torch of truth."

This body, like a clay pot, is frail and mortal,
But the soul, eternal, crosses the portal.
Many clouds pass, but the sky stays immortal,
A truth beyond death's narrow mortal.

The Fragility of the Body and Eternity of the Soul

The body, like a delicate clay vessel, is destined to fade, bound by the laws of time and mortality. Yet, the soul remains untouched, vast and eternal, like the boundless sky beyond fleeting clouds. Physical existence is but a passing moment, while the essence of the soul transcends the limits of life and death. True wisdom lies in shifting our focus from the temporary to the everlasting, nurturing the spirit over fleeting attachments. By embracing the impermanence of the body, we awaken to life's higher purpose, preparing the soul for its infinite journey beyond the confines of the mortal world.

A potter explained to his apprentice that clay pots, though beautiful, eventually break. “But,” he said, “the art and effort behind them remain eternal.” Similarly, a kind philosopher taught villagers that while their bodies are temporary, their actions and virtues endure. Years later, when the philosopher passed away, his teachings lived on, inspiring generations to focus on what truly matters—the soul’s journey and eternal impact.

Socrates, the great philosopher of ancient Athens, never wrote a single word, yet his teachings echo through the corridors of history. Condemned to death for allegedly corrupting the youth and disrespecting the gods, Socrates faced his execution with unwavering calm.

Even as he drank the poison hemlock, Socrates engaged his followers in a profound discussion about the soul’s immortality. He believed that while the body is temporary, the essence of a person—their ideas, values, and impact—lives on eternally. His students, Plato and Aristotle, carried forward his legacy, shaping Western philosophy and thought for centuries.

The story of Socrates teaches us that physical existence is fleeting, but the influence of a virtuous and impactful life endures. It reminds us to focus on cultivating wisdom, integrity, and the pursuit of truth, which transcend the limitations of mortality.

"The body fades, but the soul remains."

Man cannot choose his birth or demise,
His life's start or end are not his prize.
Why boast in the middle? It's unwise,
For fate's hand rules beyond his eyes.

The Folly of Boasting

Pride is an illusion in the grand design of existence, for neither our arrival nor departure is within our grasp. Life unfolds like a fleeting passage, with its beginning and end determined by forces beyond our control, leaving us only the present to shape with wisdom. Boasting of achievements in this brief interlude is futile, for destiny weaves the threads of fate, indifferent to human arrogance. True fulfillment lies in humility, in embracing life's transience with grace and gratitude. By surrendering to the rhythm of the universe, we find wisdom—not in dominance, but in harmony with the unseen forces that guide our journey.

A proud merchant boasted of his wealth, claiming his success was self-made. One day, a storm destroyed his ships, leaving him penniless. Seeking shelter, he met a wise monk who said, "Life's tides are beyond our control. Be humble in success, for it's a gift, not an entitlement." The merchant rebuilt his life with humility and became known for his generosity, realizing that fate, not pride, shapes our lives.

After 27 years of imprisonment under the harshest conditions, Nelson Mandela emerged not as a man filled with vengeance but as a leader committed to unity. Upon becoming South Africa's first Black president, Mandela sought to heal a deeply divided nation through reconciliation, even extending gestures of friendship to his former oppressors.

Mandela's humility in victory was profound. Despite his stature, he chose to live modestly, never allowing power to cloud his values. His ability to forgive and build bridges reflected his understanding of life's transience and the futility of arrogance.

Mandela's story serves as a powerful reminder that true greatness lies in humility. His life teaches us that enduring change is achieved not through bitterness or pride but through compassion, understanding, and a steadfast commitment to humanity.

"Pride goes before a fall."

A man cannot see his back or crown,
Nor watch his hair as it grays or browns.
Unaware of self, truth remains unknown,
For in blindness, wisdom is overthrown.

The Blindness to Truth

People often remain unaware of their own transformation—the graying of hair, the shifting of seasons, the silent passage of time—because they cannot fully see themselves. Just as one overlooks these subtle changes, those who fail to engage in deep reflection remain blind to their own nature, drifting through life without true understanding. Without self-awareness, wisdom remains distant, and existence becomes a series of unexamined moments.

True enlightenment is not found in the fleeting perceptions of the outer world but in the depths of inner exploration. Only through introspection can one strip away illusions, recognize personal flaws, and embrace growth.

It is in this journey of self-discovery that true wisdom takes root, illuminating the mind and soul. To live meaningfully, one must first have the courage to turn inward, to see oneself with clarity, and to embrace the truth that has always been waiting within.

A king who had spent his life ruling without ever looking inward, grew old and wise. One day, he asked a sage, "Why do I feel unfulfilled despite my wealth?" The sage replied, "You have ruled kingdoms, but not your own soul. Seek within to understand true wisdom." The king, now realizing his ignorance of his own heart, spent the rest of his life meditating and reflecting. He found peace not through conquest, but through self-awareness and humility. His kingdom flourished because he ruled with wisdom born from self-understanding.

In ancient Greece, the Oracle of Delphi bore the inscription, "Know Thyself." Thousands sought the oracle's wisdom, asking about their futures, fortunes, and external challenges. Yet, the true meaning of the inscription was often overlooked.

Visitors focused on their ambitions while neglecting introspection. They sought solutions in the outside world, blind to the fact that understanding themselves was the key to solving many of their problems. Philosophers like Socrates emphasized that self-awareness is the cornerstone of wisdom. To know one's strengths, flaws, and purpose is to unlock the potential for meaningful action.

The lesson of the Oracle of Delphi is timeless. In a world of distractions and external pursuits, it reminds us to turn inward. True wisdom begins not with answers but with the courage to ask, "Who am I, and what do I stand for?"

"Self-awareness is the key to wisdom."

Your body will leave, no matter your care.
Your wealth will pass to others to share.
Your life departs; none can hold it there,
For life's true riches are beyond compare.

The Impermanence of Life and Wealth

Life and all its possessions are but passing shadows, slipping through our grasp no matter how tightly we hold on. The body, no matter how well cared for, withers with time; wealth, no matter how vast, inevitably changes hands. Nothing material is truly ours, for all that we cherish in the physical world is bound to fade.

Yet, within this fleeting existence lies a treasure far greater than gold—wisdom, kindness, and the enrichment of the soul.

These are the only riches that endure, shaping not just our lives but the legacy we leave behind. True fulfillment is not found in accumulating wealth but in cultivating virtues that transcend time. When we shift our focus from the temporary to the eternal, we discover that the measure of a life well lived is not in what we possess, but in the depth of our wisdom, the love we share, and the goodness we impart to the world.

A wealthy merchant spent his life collecting gold, storing it in chests and vaults. As he grew old, he became anxious about leaving it behind. One night, he had a dream in which a wise sage told him, "Your wealth will belong to others when you leave. The only treasure that matters is your deeds and wisdom." Upon waking, the merchant decided to donate his wealth to help the poor and educate children. He spent the remainder of his life sharing knowledge and kindness, realizing that the true richness of life comes from what we give, not what we keep.

For decades, the Berlin Wall stood as a stark symbol of division, separating East and West Berlin. Families were torn apart, and freedom was curtailed by this man-made barrier. Yet, in 1989, under the weight of collective willpower, the wall crumbled, marking the end of an era.

Its fall was a powerful reminder of life's impermanence. No matter how insurmountable challenges may seem, they are but temporary. The demolition of the wall symbolized not only political change but the human spirit's ability to overcome division.

The Berlin Wall's story encourages us to remember that all barriers, whether physical or emotional, can eventually fall. It inspires hope and resilience, reminding us that change is inevitable and often within our grasp when we work together.

"You can't take your wealth with you."

Why see, why praise, why compare?
Who holds the crown in life's affair?
Is anyone greater? Does anyone care?
For greatness lies in how one dares.

The Essence of True Greatness

True greatness is not measured by wealth, power, or recognition. It lies in one's ability to act with integrity, courage, and resilience, regardless of external circumstances. Greatness is not about being above others but about having the courage to do what is right, to act according to one's values, and to rise above challenges with grace. In life's great affair, greatness comes not from external measures but from how one dares to make a difference, how one faces adversity, and how one remains humble despite success.

In a small kingdom, many sought titles, wealth, and power, believing that these were the marks of greatness. However, a humble farmer named Rajiv was known not for his riches or fame, but for his selfless contributions to his community. He worked tirelessly, helping others without seeking recognition. One day, the king visited the village and asked the people who they thought was the greatest among them. The people, in awe of Rajiv's quiet generosity, named him as the true greatest among them. The king realized that greatness was not about wealth, titles, or recognition, but about the impact one has on others and the courage to live with integrity.

Equality Among Humans

The Civil Rights Movement in the United States was a monumental struggle for racial equality and justice, driven by leaders like Martin Luther King Jr. who advocated for the fundamental truth that all humans are equal, regardless of the color of their skin or their social status. King's leadership was marked by his steadfast belief in nonviolence and peaceful protest, even in the face of violent opposition. The movement aimed to dismantle institutionalized racism and secure equal rights for African Americans, emphasizing that racial superiority, a concept deeply entrenched in society, was unjust and immoral. Through protests, legal challenges, and powerful speeches, the movement highlighted the inherent equality of all people, challenging the idea that anyone was superior or inferior based on race. King's "I Have a Dream" speech became an iconic moment in the movement, calling for a world where people would not be judged by the color of their skin but by the content of their character. The Civil Rights Movement stands as a testament to the idea that all human beings deserve equal rights and opportunities, regardless of their race, and that social constructs of superiority must be eradicated in order to build a just society.

"Greatness is not in what you have, but in what you give."

The fox tricks the lobster with its wile,
But the dog catches the fox with guile.
In life's chain, cunning walks a mile,
Yet virtue outlasts any false style.

The Price of Cunning and the Enduring Value of Virtue

In life, cunning and trickery may offer temporary success, but true virtue endures in the long run. The fox uses its wiles to trick others, but the dog catches the fox through its cleverness. While guile may win some battles, virtue—integrity, honesty, and goodness—outlasts deceit and leads to lasting success. Falsehood and trickery are fleeting, but the goodness in one's character is a powerful force that withstands time.

Once, in a dense forest, a sly fox tricked a lobster into getting caught in a trap by promising to show it the best fishing spot. However, a clever dog who had been watching from afar knew the fox's tricks. The dog followed the fox and eventually caught it, revealing the fox's deceit. The fox begged for mercy, but the dog simply said, "Cunning can win for a while, but honesty and virtue last much longer." The forest animals learned that trickery might bring short-term success, but in the end, only virtue wins respect and loyalty.

Cycle of Predation

In the natural world, the cycle of predation is an essential part of ecosystems, where the predator and prey maintain a delicate balance of survival. This cycle demonstrates the interconnectedness of all life forms, as each species relies on others for food and survival. For instance, foxes hunt smaller animals like rabbits and birds, yet they themselves can fall prey to larger predators, such as wolves or humans. This constant cycle of life and death is a fundamental part of nature, ensuring that populations remain in check and ecosystems remain balanced. However, the cycle also serves as a metaphor for human existence, reminding us that power, dominance, and survival are not permanent. Just as the fox can become prey, those who are in positions of power can find themselves vulnerable to forces beyond their control. In the same way, individuals in society who may seem dominant or invincible can eventually face their own downfall. The food chain is a natural cycle that reflects the broader dynamics of life, where every living being plays a role in maintaining the balance, and no one, whether predator or prey, is exempt from the laws of nature.

"Deceit may fool for a while, but virtue wins in the end."

Curd can't revert to milk again,
But milk turns curd, and so remain.
The fool can't grasp wisdom's gain,
For only the willing will break the chain.

The Fool's Inability to Understand Wisdom

Just as curd cannot be returned to milk, a fool cannot undo their ignorance through mere effort. Wisdom cannot be forced onto someone unwilling to learn or change. While milk can turn into curd through a natural process, the transformation from ignorance to wisdom requires openness, humility, and the willingness to break free from mental chains. A fool will remain unchanged until they choose to seek knowledge and understanding.

A wise sage was once approached by a young man who sought to learn. The sage gave him a task: "You must turn this curd back into milk." The young man, puzzled, tried many ways but failed. The sage smiled and said, "Just as curd cannot return to milk, a fool cannot grasp wisdom if he is not willing to change. Wisdom comes to those who are willing to learn, not those who resist growth." The young man, humbled, began his journey of true learning, understanding that wisdom requires more than just effort—it requires an open heart and mind.

Irreversible Change

The Industrial Revolution, which began in the late 18th century, is one of history's most transformative events, reshaping economies and societies in ways that are still felt today. With the advent of machines, factories, and new technologies, industries that once relied on manual labor became mechanized, increasing production capacity exponentially. The revolution altered the course of human history, leading to urbanization, changes in labor systems, and the rise of new economic powers. However, the shift to industrialization also marked the beginning of irreversible changes. The transition from agrarian societies to urban centers, from handcrafts to mass production, could not be undone. This profound shift had far-reaching effects on social structures, family life, and the environment. The rapid growth of factories led to overcrowded cities, poor working conditions, and environmental degradation. Despite these negative consequences, industrialization ultimately propelled human progress, leading to modern technologies, innovations, and economic growth. Yet, like the transformation of milk into curd, some changes are permanent. The Industrial Revolution serves as a powerful reminder that some transitions, once made, cannot be reversed, and that the effects of those changes are felt across generations.

"Wisdom cannot be forced upon the unwilling."

Chapter 18

Miscellaneous Concepts

Life is an intricate balance of emotions, choices, and experiences. While individual concepts shape thoughts and actions, they are interconnected. Wisdom comes from seeing the larger picture, where every lesson complements another. Understanding one value leads to insights into many others. The journey of self-awareness involves exploring diverse ideas, each offering a unique perspective. In the grand scheme, no single concept exists in isolation; rather, they weave together to form a complete understanding of life. Reflection, curiosity, and open-mindedness lead to deeper awareness and a more fulfilling existence. Beyond these themes, history offers countless lessons—from the importance of art and culture to the unpredictability of fate. The human story is ever-unfolding, shaped by philosophy, action, and the pursuit of meaning.

The fish glides freely in water's embrace,
But flounders helpless on land's face.
Its strength lies not in itself, but its place,
For wisdom lies in knowing one's space.

Know Your Place

Like a fish that flourishes in water but struggles on land, every individual thrives when they understand their true nature and limitations. Strength is not about pushing beyond one's essence but about recognizing where one's abilities can be best applied. Just as a misplaced fish is doomed to perish, a person who ignores their strengths and blindly chases an unsuitable path invites failure.

True wisdom lies in self-awareness—knowing where one belongs, embracing one's unique talents, and working within that space to achieve greatness. Success is not found in reckless ambition but in the mastery of one's own role. By aligning with our natural abilities rather than resisting them, we create a path of fulfillment, purpose, and lasting achievement.

A young bird, eager to soar, watched the fish swimming gracefully in the pond. Wishing to be like the fish, the bird dived into the water but found itself floundering. A wise old turtle saw the bird struggling and said, "You must know your place. The fish thrives in water, but your strength lies in the air." The bird realized that its wings were meant for flight, not for swimming. It took the turtle's advice to heart and learned to embrace its unique strengths. Wisdom is knowing where you excel and respecting your nature.

Strength of Context

Amelia Earhart, one of the most celebrated pioneers in aviation, was known for her daring flights and remarkable achievements, breaking barriers in a male-dominated field. However, her final flight in 1937, which led to her mysterious disappearance over the Pacific Ocean, highlighted the critical role that context plays in success. While Earhart was an exceptional pilot, capable of navigating various challenges, she faced extreme conditions that were beyond her control. Adverse weather, mechanical issues, and navigation errors compounded by limited resources during her flight made her task increasingly difficult. The circumstances surrounding her last journey ultimately proved that even the most skilled individuals are vulnerable when the context is unfavorable. Earhart's story serves as a reminder that success is not solely determined by an individual's abilities, but also by the circumstances surrounding their efforts. It is easy to overlook the influence of external factors on achievement, but the challenges she faced show that context—be it weather, timing, or resources—can be just as pivotal as one's skill and determination. Earhart's disappearance is a testament to the fact that even the greatest achievements can be undermined by circumstances beyond one's control.

"Know thyself."

A goldsmith skilled in his artful trade
Fears no famine; his wealth is made.
Know your craft, and be unafraid,
For true value is found in what you've laid.

The Power of Mastery and Self-Sufficiency

A skilled artisan, like a goldsmith, knows that the true source of wealth lies in expertise and craftsmanship. Such individuals are not afraid of external hardships, such as famine, because they possess the ability to create value through their talents. Mastery in one's craft is a form of independence—when you are proficient in something, you can navigate through any adversity with confidence. True wealth is not always in material possession but in the skills you develop and apply in life.

Once, there was a goldsmith who lived in a small village. Despite the challenges of famine and economic downturn, he never feared hunger or poverty. While many around him struggled, he used his craft to make beautiful jewelry, which he traded for food. People asked him how he survived the hard times, and he replied, "My skill is my wealth. As long as I have this, I will never fear any famine." His wisdom was evident: in mastering a trade and honing his skills, he had secured a form of wealth that no calamity could take away.

Skill as a Lifeline

Marie Curie's legacy is a testament to the power of skill and knowledge in shaping one's destiny. As a pioneer in the field of radioactivity, she not only advanced the study of physics and chemistry but also broke barriers for women in science. Curie's unparalleled expertise in these fields led to groundbreaking discoveries, including the isolation of radium and polonium, and she became the first woman to win a Nobel Prize. Her mastery in these areas was not just an academic achievement—it became a lifeline. During a time when women were often excluded from the scientific community, Curie's skills earned her recognition and respect, even in the face of societal biases. The knowledge she gained through her studies allowed her to chart her own path in an otherwise male-dominated world. Marie Curie's career highlights the value of mastering one's craft and how expertise in a field can not only lead to independence but also leave a lasting impact on the world. Her story shows that with skill and determination, even the most daunting barriers can be overcome, and one's work can lead to profound change and recognition.

"Master your craft, and the world will never leave you empty-handed."

To bear a son is a hopeful aim,
Generations strive to build their name.
But do sons always uphold their claim?
For legacy is earned, not simply a fame.

The True Nature of Legacy

While many seek to leave behind a legacy, it is not enough to simply have a son or heirs to carry on one's name. Legacy is built on the actions, values, and wisdom passed down through generations, not just on familial ties. Sons may not always live up to the expectations set by their ancestors. True legacy is earned through the deeds and qualities of those who carry it forward, and it is established through the choices made by each individual, not by their mere birthright.

A nobleman, proud of his family lineage, often boasted, "My sons will carry my name and my legacy forward." However, over the years, his sons failed to uphold the values he had cherished. They were selfish and indifferent to the responsibilities of their family name. One day, a wise elder spoke to him, "Legacy is not inherited by birth, but by the actions of the heart. You may have sons, but only they can shape their legacy." The nobleman came to understand that a true legacy is not about bloodline, but about the character and actions that define one's life.

Hope for Progeny

Throughout history, many dynasties and empires placed great emphasis on ensuring the survival of their lineage, often prioritizing heirs to carry on their legacy. Kings and emperors believed that having a successor was essential to maintaining political stability and preserving their family's power. However, the hope for progeny did not always yield the desired results. Many rulers faced struggles in producing heirs, and even when they did, the successors often failed to live up to the expectations placed upon them. Some were too young, inexperienced, or lacked the necessary qualities to govern effectively. Others fell victim to court intrigues, rebellions, or personal weaknesses. Despite these challenges, rulers continued to focus on securing their legacy through their children, understanding that dynasties were often only as strong as the rulers who succeeded them. The history of dynastic succession shows how the pursuit of an heir, while crucial to the survival of empires, can also bring its own set of complications. The pressure to produce a worthy successor highlights the delicate balance between ambition, legacy, and the unpredictable nature of human capability.

"Legacy is earned, not inherited."

Epilogue

As this journey through philosophy and life's principles comes to a close, the essence of wisdom remains—ever-evolving, ever-relevant. The reflections in these chapters are not meant to provide final answers but to open doors to deeper thought and self-awareness.

Life is a constant dialogue between the known and the unknown, the transient and the eternal. The greatest insights often come not from certainty, but from the willingness to question, adapt, and grow. As you step beyond these pages, may you carry forward the understanding that knowledge deepens through practice, wisdom flourishes through experience, and truth reveals itself to those who seek it with an open mind.

This is not an end but a beginning—an invitation to continue exploring, learning, and shaping your own path toward a meaningful and enlightened life.

About The Author

R.P. Sidgen is a thinker, writer, and seeker of wisdom, deeply passionate about exploring the philosophical principles that shape human existence. With a keen interest in the intersections of ethics, history, and human nature, Sidgen's writings reflect a profound understanding of life's timeless truths.

Blending deep introspection with clarity, An Ethical Compass is a testament to Sidgen's belief that philosophy is not merely a subject of study but a way of living—a guide that helps us navigate the complexities of our inner and outer worlds.

Beyond writing, Sidgen is dedicated to learning, teaching, and sharing insights that inspire self-reflection and meaningful change. This book is an invitation to readers to embark on a journey of thought, discovery, and transformation.

For more insights, reflections, and updates, connect with the author at: admin@sidgenbooks.com

www.ingramcontent.com/pod-product-compliance
Ingram Content Group UK Ltd.
Pitfield, Milton Keynes, MK11 3LW, UK
UKHW041346190726
13845UKWH00026B/453

9 789334 279511